∴ A la Cart

TAMALES—(Beef) Chile Sauce 30c

ENCHILADA (Cheese and Onions) 35c

ENCHILADA (Beef) 40c
(With Fried Egg — 5c Extra)

ENCHILADA (With Beans, Rice or Spaghetti) 40c

CHILE RELLENO 35c

TOSTADA 35c

SPANISH EGG OMELETTE 45c

SPANISH SAUSAGE WITH EGGS 50c

CHILE CON CARNE 35c

CHILE CON CARNE (With Rice and Beans
    or Spaghetti) 35c

CHILE BEANS 25c

FRIED BEANS WITH CHEESE 30c

SPANISH RICE 35c

MEXICAN SPAGHETTI 35c

HAMBURGER STEAK, with Chile Beans,
    Spaghetti and French Fried Potatoes 40c

GREEN CORN TAMALES (In Season) 35c

TORTILLAS { CORN TORTILLAS OR BREAD INCLUDED WITH MEALS

MILK OR TOASTED CORN TORTILLAS — 5c EXTRA

EL CHOLO COOKBOOK

EL CHOLO COOKBOOK

Recipes and Lore

from California's

Best-Loved

Mexican Kitchen

. . . .

Merrill Shindler

ANGEL CITY PRESS
1998

ANGEL CITY PRESS, INC.
2118 Wilshire Boulevard, Suite 880
Santa Monica, California 90403
(310) 395-9982
http://www.angelcitypress.com

First published in 1998 by Angel City Press
3 5 7 9 10 8 6 4 2

ISBN 1-883318-11-4

El Cholo Cookbook
By Merrill Shindler

Design and illustrations by Dave Matli.
Photographs on pages 42 & 43 copyright © 1998 by David G. McAuley

Library of Congress Cataloging-in-Publication Data

Shindler, Merrill Karsh, 1948-

    El Cholo cookbook : recipes and memories from California's
        best-loved Mexican kitchen / by Merrill Shindler and the El Cholo
        Family. — 1st ed.
            144 p. : ill. ; 26 cm.
            Includes index.
            ISBN 1-883318-11-4 (cloth)
            1. Cookery, Mexican. 2. Cookery — California. 3. El Cholo
    (Restaurant) — History. I. El Cholo (Restaurant) II. Title.
    TX716.M4 S46 1998
    641.5/0979494—dc20   98-8917
                                                                CIP

Printed in Hong Kong

A mi esposa Merri y mi perro Jed – gracias para todo.
— Merrill Shindler

*To my mom and dad who set the standard and imbued the passion, and
to Roslyn Smith who created the beauty and charm.*
— Ron Salisbury

And especially to Jose Cuervo with whom we formed a partner-
ship in 1967 to create the best margarita in the world. It is the
standard by which El Cholo is judged.   —R. S.

·Acknowledgments·

My thanks to Ron Salisbury and his remarkable family and staff, not only for opening their lives to me, but for several decades of the best Mexican cooking served in the best city in the United States for eating Mexican food. All I needed to inspire me to dig deeper and to write more was to think of El Cholo's sublime Green Corn Tamales, a dish worthy of an epic poem all its own, and of the restaurant's landmark margaritas, the finest fuel a writer could want.
— **Merrill Shindler**

I sincerely hope that you will enjoy reading about El Cholo's history, and sharing the passion that's been the basis for being in business more than seventy years. I am extremely grateful to Merrill Shindler for telling our story so well.

The restaurant business provides some very special opportunities. You share a very close, common bond with some wonderful individuals and amazing people come into your life, some of whom will become your closest friends. I'm living proof of this. Being in the restaurant business has given me lifelong friendships I might never have enjoyed otherwise.

I want to pay tribute to those who formed my early understanding and attitude about this business. First, my mom, who endowed me with the absolutely necessary passion. And, of course, my dad, who taught me that ninety-nine percent isn't good enough, and that there's no substitute for the best.

To Carl Anders, who reminded me that even if you own five restaurants, you aren't too good to get your hands wet washing dishes, and that if your intuition tells you something will work, trust it, even though others will tell you it won't – then make it happen.

From Rudi Monterastelli, I learned how to make sure that after you sell a dinner, you make sure that you retain a modest profit that enables you to open the door the next day.

And thanks to Randy Randazzo, who showed me how you can have a great time doing what you do and how to enjoy your guests.

Last, but certainly not least, my loving gratitude to my Aunt Blanche March, who at the age of ninety-three wanted to buy the property next to her restaurant and build to-go facilities because she felt "that is the wave of the future."

To all those, and so many more, I offer my thanks.
— **Ron Salisbury**

-Contents-

EL CHOLO: THE HERITAGE

SETTING THE SCENE: LOS ANGELES IN THE TWENTIES

El Cholo was born in 1927, a year of great prosperity and grand optimism. Indeed, El Cholo wasn't the only culinary innovation that appeared that year that has affected our lives in deep and notable ways. Just consider, for a moment, the wonders that emerged in 1927 – not the least of which was Wonder Bread, introduced that year in its trademark multicolored balloon-adorned wrapper by the Continental Baking Company. Continental also introduced Hostess Cakes that year, those wonderful little chocolate piles topped with a hard chocolate frosting with a distinctive squiggle upon it.

It was also the birth year of Lender's Bagels, which would in time become America's largest bagel baker – and the creator (for better or worse) of the flash-frozen bagel. It was the year that the world took its first taste of B&M Brick Oven Baked Beans, produced by Burham & Morrill of Portland, Maine. Gerber Baby Foods were born that year, thanks to a Fremont, Michigan, food processor named Daniel F. Gerber, who began to feed his daughter Sally strained peas on the advice of her doctor. He was shocked to find that strained baby food was available only by prescription at pharmacies, at prices that were shocking. His desire to create a lower-priced baby food changed the way infants would eat for the rest of the century.

An Austrian company put out a line of peppermint breath mints in 1927, intended at first to sooth the raw throats of smokers. The name of the mints came from the German word for peppermint, *pfefferminz*, which they condensed to Pez. Both Mike & Ike and Hot Tamales came on the market, and became overnight sensations. A Hastings, Nebraska, inventor named Edward E. Perkins came up with the idea of turning the bulky liquid Fruit-Smack drink concentrates he'd been marketing into an easier-to-transport powdered product that could easily be reconstituted with the simple addition of water and ice. He called it Kool-Aid. At the Laurentian Dairy in Ottawa, Canada, homogenized milk was sold for the first time to the public, who took to it like proverbial fish to water. They also drank Welch-Ade for the first time, a carbonated grape drink that wasn't champagne. And speaking of champagne, it was in 1927 that the French Parliament passed a law decreeing that only wine bottled in the region called Champagne could properly be called Champagne. All others, by law, had to be referred to as sparkling wine.

In terms of restaurants, along with El Cholo, 1927 was the year the original Les Frères Taix opened in Los Angeles, down at 321 Commercial Street (it's currently at 1911 Sunset Boulevard), opened by the Taix family as a clever outlet for "medicinal wines" (it was Prohibition, after all), served along with many of the dishes still on the menu – escargots, trout amandine and the like, costing a people-pleasing forty cents for lunch and fifty cents for dinner.

Not far away, the Mayflower Hotel (now called Checkers) opened with Ye Bull Pen Restaurant on the ground floor, a theme eatery where diners have to make their way through piles of straw strewn across the concrete floor to reach "stalls" brightened by coal-oil lamps, where they consume dollar-and-fifty-cent planked steaks in a setting intended to be reminiscent of a cattle shed. An odd concept, dining in the last home of the beast whose flesh you're consuming, but very popular at the time.

Around the country, restaurants were opening with remarkable rapidity. The first of Marriott's Hot Shoppes opened in Washington, D.C., a nine-seat A&W Root Beer stand that would eventually grow into one of the biggest restaurant chains in America. (Interestingly, the original menu featured chili con carne and hot tamales.) In Boston, the Ritz Hotel

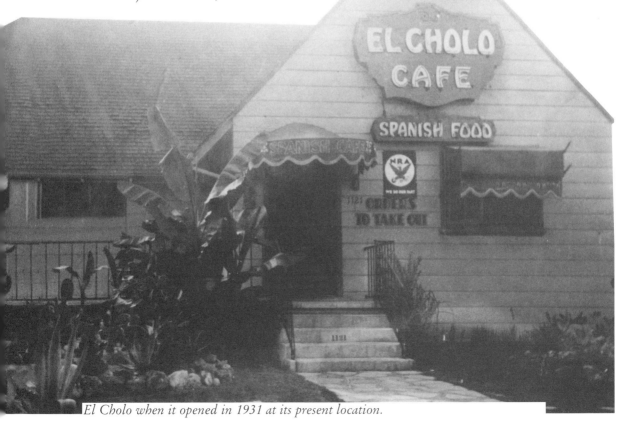

El Cholo when it opened in 1931 at its present location.

Alejandro   and   Rosa Borquez

Aurelia   and   George Salisbury

opened, serving scrod in its dining room. In New York, the Russian Tea Room began life just to the left of Carnegie Hall, more as a soda fountain than a Russian restaurant. Vodka, of course, will not appear on the menu until after Prohibition. And in Paris, La Coupole opened on the Boulevard du Montparnasse, serving *escargots de Bourgogne, choucroute Alsacienne* and *cassoulet d'oie Toulousain.*

As a point of further context, in 1924, a year after the birth of the original El Cholo (which was actually called Sonora Cafe when it opened), the *sine qua non* of American salads was born on a hot, dusty Fourth of July weekend at Caesar Cardini's Caesar's Palace restaurant in Tijuana, Mexico. Supposedly, on this particular busy weekend, Cardini was running low on food. And so, staring into his icebox, he tossed together a salad for his guests from what was left over. The Caesar Salad quickly traveled north of the border, and turned into a hallmark of tony dining establishments, where it was usually made at table side with many a flourish and grand gesture. Bottles of Cardini's Original Caesar Dressing can be found to this day in better markets.

Just one year before El Cholo, the Brown Derby opened in Hollywood, a restaurant destined to give the world the Cobb Salad. Like the Caesar, the story of the salad claims that enterprising restaurateur Bob Cobb gazed forlornly into his diminished larder, then cleverly cobbled together what would become a legendary dish made with the assiduous use of leftovers. The original Cobb, created in 1926, wasn't so much diced as it was pulverized, turned into a sort of culinary dust. It had no texture except for a vague grittiness. It was a great dish for people without teeth.

If there was a culinary theme that ran through the restaurants of Los Angeles in the 1920s, it wasn't toothlessness. It was the golden age of the cafeteria, especially the six Boos Brothers Cafeterias (the fabled Clifton Cafeterias didn't come along until 1931). According to historian Bruce Henstell, in his fine volume *Sunshine and Wealth: Los Angeles in the Twenties and Thirties*, "The flagship installation was on Hill Street, across from Pershing Square. It was designed 'in the quaint style of English inns of 200 years ago,' which must have made it look right at home in downtown Los Angeles. It had half-timbered work inside, wrought-iron lanterns, subdued light although not candles, and a foyer outside the restrooms fit for barons and earls."

It was an age of the Cocoanut Grove and the Zinnia Grill. Of Carl Jahnke's Coffee Shop and John Tait's Coffee Shop. Of Frank Sebastian's Cotton Club and the Victor Hugo. There were lines nightly at Philippe the Original and the Original Pantry Cafe. Meat was consumed in quantity at Musso & Frank, the Pacific Dining Car, the Derby and the Tam O'Shanter. Deli was found at Greenblatt's and Canter's. And in 1927, a new standard was set for Mexican food at a small cafe called El Cholo.

EL CHOLO: HISTORY IN EVERY BITE

The roots of El Cholo can be traced back to 1922, when Alejandro Borquez told his wife Rosa, "You are such a good cook; we should open up a restaurant." Out of such simple statements are legends born. In 1923, Alejandro and Rosa opened a restaurant in downtown Los Angeles, named the Sonora Cafe, not far from the Los Angeles Coliseum, where the menu proudly proclaimed that the cooking was "Spanish-Mexican." The menu back then was the very essence of simplicity – albondigas soup (described on the menu as "Spanish meatball soup") and vegetable soup; salads of sliced tomatoes, hearts of lettuce and "Mexican pickled peppers;" all of eight entrees (beef tamale, cheese or beef enchiladas, chile relleno, tostada, chili con carne, fried beans with cheese, Spanish rice); and a combina-

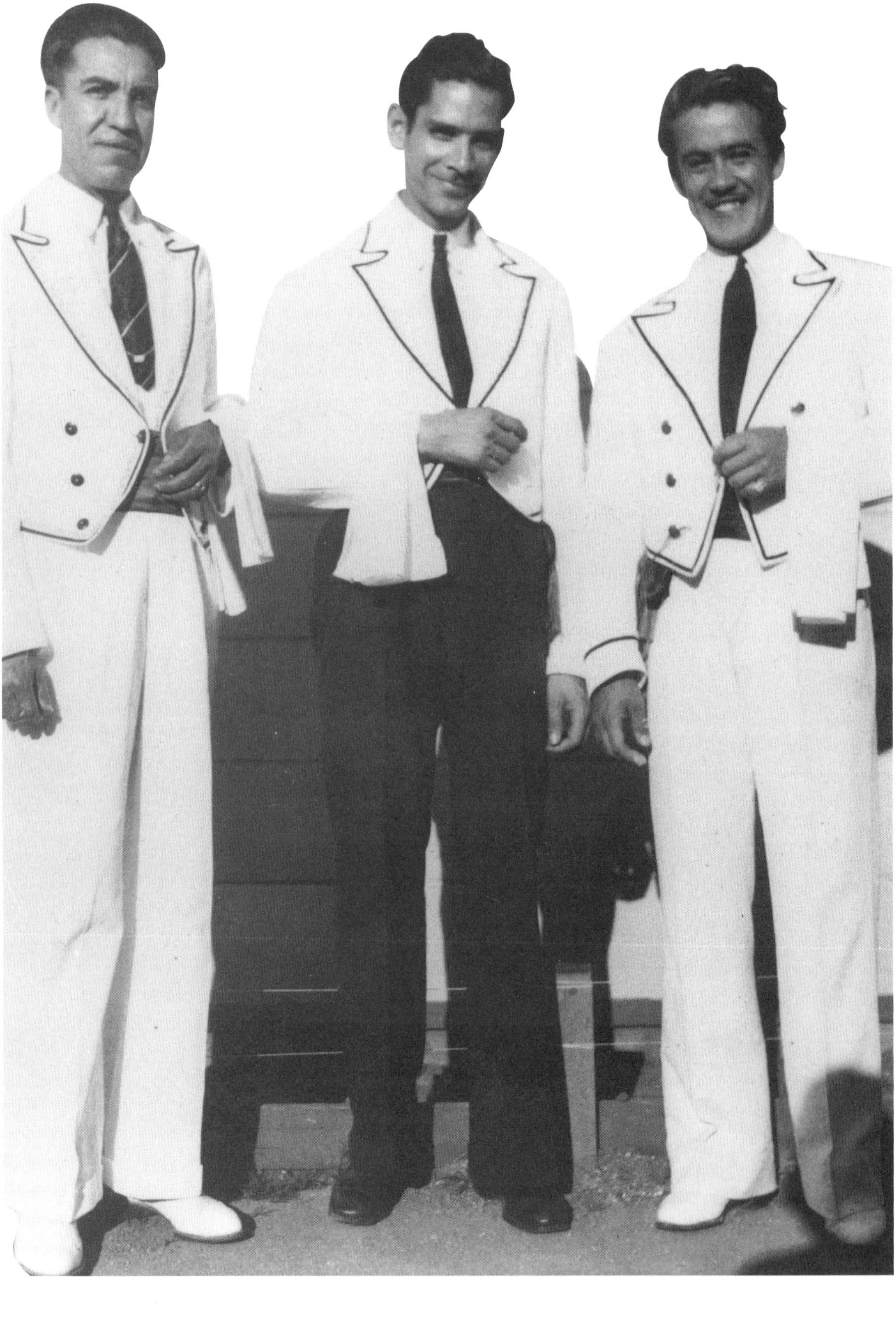

tion plate of an enchilada, a chile relleno, a tamale, chile con carne, fried beans and rice. The clientele reflected the current population of Los Angeles (much as it does today); at any given time, there was a range of diners that would go from immigrants hungry for a taste of home, to businessmen grabbing a quick lunch, to shoppers enjoying the stylish stores that were a big attraction in the downtown area seven decades ago. The attraction for all was simple – big portions of tasty food served at reasonable prices. Once again, much as it is today.

Over the past seventy years, El Cholo has became a popular carousing spot for University of Southern California students after football games at the nearby Coliseum. It also became a major watering hole for Hollywood luminaries such as Bing Crosby, Clark Gable, Irving Berlin, Jack Nicholson, Warren Beatty, Madonna, Marlon Brando, Elizabeth Taylor, George Hamilton, David Letterman and His Honor Mayor Richard Riordan, who have journeyed to Western Avenue to eat tamales, chiles rellenos, enchiladas, and drink margaritas.

Today, the restaurant is run by Ron Salisbury (son of George and Aurelia) and his family, forming an unbroken chain back to the original owners. (Salisbury has further honored his family heritage by opening a new Sonora Cafe in the heart of Los Angeles, serving upscale Southwestern dishes. The name, like El Cholo, has been passed on from generation to generation.) The food at El Cholo gives us a fair idea of what Mexican cooking was like in Southern California more than seventy years ago, back in the days when it was referred as "Spanish cuisine." (The original neon sign at El Cholo still says "Spanish Cafe" on it.)

The history of El Cholo actually begins in Arizona, rather than in Mexico. Aurelia Borquez, mother of Ron Salisbury, was born in the tiny town of Globe, Arizona. His father, George Salisbury, was born in equally small Safford, Arizona – two little towns down the road from each other. Both families moved to Los Angeles when Aurelia and George were in their teens, although they had not met yet. Aurelia's parents, Alejandro and Rosa Borquez were almost in their forties when they decided to open their first restaurant in downtown Los Angeles on Broadway."

That was the original Sonora Cafe. But it didn't keep that name for long. In 1925, a guest walked in and while he was waiting, he absentmindedly doodled on a menu. He drew a figure of a Mexican peasant, and over the picture wrote the words "El Cholo." Aurelia Borquez saw the drawing, and asked if she could have it. She took it to her dad who liked it so much that he immediately changed the name of the restaurant to El Cholo and used the drawing of the peasant as the logo. El Cholo was born.

Shortly after that, George Salisbury came into the restaurant, met Aurelia, and, in the terminology of the age, began keeping company with her. Inspired by the growing success and reputation of El Cholo, they opened their own branch at 1107 S. Western Avenue in another small storefront in 1927. They were married soon after, in 1929. In 1931, El Cholo moved across the street to its current location. Interestingly, George and Aurelia were warned by more than a few friends and customers that moving across the street would be a mistake. The doomsayers were wrong. As of 1997, the restaurant celebrated its seventieth year across the street.

What's now El Cholo was originally a small house, a California bungalow that was expanded, over the years, into the surprisingly large restaurant, bar and party room that it is today. Elements of the original house are still there – the area to the left of the hostess stand was originally an outdoor patio. The comfortable room adjacent to the bar was the living room; the fireplace from the original living room remains. What's now a long dining room was once two bedrooms with a bathroom in the middle. Changes didn't happen overnight; back in the thirties and forties that bathroom, then the ladies' restroom, still had a bathtub in it. And the kitchen door was always open so people could look in. There was a perception that Mexican cooking techniques weren't sanitary, and the Salisburys wanted people to be able to look into the kitchen and see their dedication to cleanliness.

Though El Cholo didn't singlehandedly popularize Mexican cooking in Los Angeles, it was in the forefront of the handful of eateries that made Mexican dishes all the rage in the 1930s. Immigrants knew about the food. But it was Anglos, newly educated to the joys of tacos and enchiladas, who queued up nightly in front of El Cholo on Western, forming a long line that would go down the sidewalk and bend around the corner. As Ron Salisbury points out, "It was the best advertising possible. We were packed all the time."

In a short time, El Cholo became the place of choice – the Spago of its age. The rich residents of Hancock Park would be driven over in their chauffeured limousines. Prominent city leaders became regulars. And it's worth noting that they were spending about eighty cents for a full meal. Many an evening, El Cholo could claim much the same clientele as expensive and very posh Perino's a few blocks away, where a cup of coffee alone was a dollar.

The success of El Cholo inspired the birth of more restaurants. In 1931, Ron's aunt and uncle opened El Coyote, which still exists, filled nightly with legions of students from UCLA and USC, who live on a diet of combination plates and margaritas. "They had a bar before we did, dating back to the forties," Salisbury remembers. "They were on La Brea Avenue for a long time, but moved in the fifties to Beverly Boulevard, to what used to be called McDonald's. It had nothing to do with the hamburger chain. It was McDonald's Monterey. When it became available, they bought it. And again people told them they were crazy to move."

But despite the appearance of spinoffs, the major destination for Mexican food in Los Angeles was El Cholo. And as most institutions will, El Cholo attracted a fair number of colorful characters – both working and eating there.

One of the most memorable was Joe Reina. In 1932, just five years after El Cholo opened, Joe Reina came

60¢ Combination Plate
SOUP
Albondigas or Vegetable
Choice of One
ENCHILADA
CHILE RELLENO   TAMALE
CHILE CON CARNE
with
FRIED BEANS
and
RICE or SPAGHETTI
TORTILLAS or BREAD
Coffee or Milk
Glass Beer   Glass Claret

45¢ 12:00 to 3:00 P.M. Special Plate Lunch
VEGETABLE SOUP
Choice of One:
ENCHILADA   TAMALE
CHILE CON CARNE
with
FRIED BEANS
and
RICE or SPAGHETTI
TORTILLAS or BREAD
Coffee
Glass Beer   Glass Claret

From El Cholo's 1927 menu.

to work as a dishwasher. But he wasn't destined to wash dishes for long. He showed great promise as a cook, and after a brief apprenticeship, became head chef. He held that job for the next fifty-four years – until he died at seventy. During that time, the number of meals he cooked easily numbered in the hundreds of thousands and most of his recipes continue to be served today. As Ron Salisbury recalls, "Joe Reina set the El Cholo standard. In fact, Joe's cooking and presentation became the standard by which most Mexican restaurants have judged themselves."

But there were others who shaped the future. Ron remembers Nacho, too: "Back in the early days it was a six-day work week. I grew up during that period and I remember working for my dad for ten dollars a day. I was working summertimes and after school sorting dishes. Restaurants don't sort dishes anymore. But my dad believed if you sorted dishes they wouldn't chip. For many, many years we had an old dishwasher named Nacho, who couldn't speak English. He always showed up on time, never missed a day. Whenever he left his station it was spotless. When he finally retired, I found out that Nacho had bought ten homes and was living very comfortably. What a great success story."

When El Cholo reopened in 1946, after being briefly shuttered to help the war effort during World War II, Reymundo Vicente applied for the singular busboy job at the restaurant. And from 1946 until 1963, he remained the restaurant's only busboy. As the quintessential service person, he didn't just do his job – he also served beer and wine to guests waiting in the lounge for dinner, wrapped all the takeout orders, and even did the maintenance work around the restaurant in his off-hours. In 1963, he became a waiter. And in 1996, Reymundo celebrated his fiftieth year with El Cholo – a half century of making service an art.

But as colorful as the workers may be, the customers have made El Cholo what it is. Ron Salisbury remembers: "There was a family by the name of Love who came in regularly. They had great-looking, nice kids, and one of them was named Mike. I remember he was about twenty years old, when I asked him, 'What are you doing now?' He told me, 'My cousins and I have formed a singing group and we're trying to make some records.' I thought to myself, what a shame, how disappointed his parents must be, and this poor kid will be so disillusioned.' Of course, that group was the Beach Boys."

Then there's the story of Tom Morey. Tom wasn't a Beach Boy. But his is a beach boy story. He was one of the many USC students who made El Cholo their home away from home. The way Ron tells it, Tom would come in barefoot, looking like a poor, bedraggled kid who had to be reminded to please put on his shoes. He eventually moved to Hawaii. While there he created the hugely successful Morey Boogie Board. Ron says, "He went on to become someone who sold millions of his boogie boards. I called him up, and told him he was a folk hero. Now, we've got an autographed picture of him in the lobby."

One of Ron's favorite stories is about John O'Melveny, the very prominent attorney: "Mr. O'Melveny sometimes would come in with his friend, Jack Winston. Mr. O'Melveny was an outstanding tipper. And when the subject of the check came up, they'd go back and forth, with the waiters hoping that Mr. O'Melveny would get the check because there was quite a difference in the tip that they'd get from Mr. O'Melveny and the one they'd get from Mr. Winston. Mr. Winston was slow on the draw when it came to getting his wallet. There was a waitress who always said, 'When I see Mr. O'Melveny coming through that door, all I can see is a five-dollar tip.' As a man-

Making tortillas in Los Angeles, circa 1927 (Courtesy Los Angeles Public Library).

ager, I had to seat him in a different place every time, to spread him around so everybody had a chance to make those five dollars – which was more than the entire bill."

Then there was actor Jack Nicholson. El Cholo was virtually a second home to Jack and his friends. "They came in often and ordered the least expensive item on the menu, the two tacos and beans for seventy-five cents, and coffee for a dime. They were all trying to break into the movies. As a group of young actors, they'd sit around for hours, talking about making it. I remember once I was working the cash register, and Jack started talking pure gibberish to some of his friends. He didn't make a bit of sense; he was acting, but I was spellbound. Even though he wasn't saying anything, I hung on every word. He was totally engaging saying nothing."

There's more to the saga of Jack Nicholson and El Cholo. "I remember he came in one night about quarter past ten, we had just closed. He walked up to the hostess and she told him we were closed. He said, 'All I want is my enchilada, rice and beans.' She said, 'Sorry we're closed.' Once again, he said, 'All I want is my enchilada, rice and beans.' He said it ten times in a row. Finally the manager came out and served him. It was a lesson in passion – he wanted it and he was going to get it."

Life hasn't been all chips and salsa, though. There was the memorable day in 1928 that someone tried to rob the place. "It was back when my dad first opened. The holdup man came in and took the money, forty dollars, which was a fortune in those days. He then ran out the front of the building, and my dad ran out the back, into the alley, and they bumped into each other. The man put a gun in my dad's face, and told him to back off. The robber jumped in a car and drove off. So my dad commandeered a car whose owner was in the drugstore on the corner. He took off and chased the theif across Washington Boulevard, across Venice Boulevard. Cars were careening; it was like something out of a *Keystone Kops* movie. Finally, the robber crashed his car over near Washington and Normandie Avenue. That's when the police showed up, chased him into the park and caught him. So my dad got his money back."

There's also the story of the man who was found guilty of armed robbery. The judge asked him why he did what he did. And he said he needed the money to buy margaritas at El Cholo and prime rib at Lawry's.

El Cholo hasn't had a long relationship just with the city of

Los Angeles; there's a special relationship with the police as well. "A few years back, we felt the morale of the police department was down. We wanted them to know that people appreciate what they're trying to do. We asked if we could do anything to send a positive message. The department told us we could buy a computer, or a desk for them. That didn't seem like the sort of gesture that would mean anything. While I was thinking about it, a police car drove by. And I came up with the idea of selling twenty-two thousand raffle tickets, for a dollar each, at the restaurant and buying a police car with the money. When all the tickets were sold, the winner would own El Cholo for a day. It was an opportunity to fulfill a fantasy that many people have to 'run' the restaurant and keep the profits for the day. The winner was a lady who lived out in San Bernardino. And the police got a brand new squad car."

El Cholo, in other words, isn't just a place to eat. It's part of the culture in Los Angeles – and has been for seven decades now. Ron Salisbury, speaking for his whole family, says, "To me, El Cholo is a cross-section of what Los Angeles is really about. We have people coming in Rolls Royces and people taking the bus. We have students, wealthy people, people who are barely getting along, and yes, some struggling actors. You name it, they come here. To me that's always been a part of the charm."

In a way, at El Cholo, it all boils down to family. Indeed, it's family that Ron Salisbury always comes back to. "It was my mom and dad who were truly my mentors – they taught me about the passion, the love of this restaurant, that hopefully will continue on in future generations. I'm very, very fortunate that I have sons who want to see this restaurant continue on, and I'm hopeful that what it represents will be here when I'm long gone. And I know the next generation is taken care of. I like to admit that my children have really far surpassed me. They do things that I never dreamed of doing."

MEXICAN COOKING: ROOTS AND ORIGINS

chapter 2

MEXICAN COOKING: ROOTS AND ORIGINS

For seven decades, El Cholo has been the bellwether for Mexican food not just in Southern California, but in America – the paragon against which all other orders of nachos, margaritas, guacamole, tamales, burritos, enchiladas, and tacos are judged. It's a reminder of just how complex, exceptional and multilayered this ancient cuisine can be. And it's also a reminder of how little respect the colorful cooking of Mexico receives. The cuisine at El Cholo raises the question of why Mexican cooking has long been the Rodney Dangerfield of cuisines – the cuisine that restaurant critics just don't take all that seriously.

Just consider: In George Christy's 1970 guide to inexpensive eats in Los Angeles, The *Los Angeles Underground Gourmet*, among several hundred reasonably priced, ethnic, downhome restaurants, a mere eight Mexican eateries are listed – Barragan Cafe, El Coyote, El Paseo Inn, El Poche Cafe, La Cantina, Pepe's, Por Favor and Señor Pico (most of which have long departed for that great mariachi bar in the sky). Strangely, El Cholo doesn't make the Underground Gourmet list, though since being on that list seemed to guarantee a brief life span, that's probably a good thing.

Prior to the birth of El Cholo in 1927, Mexican cooking existed in a sort of shadow zone somewhere between nonexistence and culinary novelty. In the definitive, encyclopedic *Eating in America: A History* by Waverley Root & Richard de Rochemont, a book that covers at great length every ethnic contribution to the cooking of the United State, the Mexican part of that contribution consists of just one-half of one paragraph. In speaking about American eating habits in the 1840s, they almost offhandedly note that: "Mexican dishes began to have some popularity, notably in the southern cities, and added a variety of format and flavors. Somehow, tamales of cornmeal, chopped meat and hot pepper, wrapped in a cornhusk and steamed, had more to offer than hoecake, johnnycake or pone. Chili con carne, which Mexicans repudiate as not being part of their cuisine, and Texans vaunt as part of theirs, had not yet arrived on the scene in any of its 'Tex-Mex' forms, but Texans adopted other Mexican ways of cooking eggs and meat, as has the whole Southwest in our times." Compared with the contributions at the time of the French and the British, Mexican cooking was just a footnote.

A bit further on, Root and de Rochemont mention, in between waxing poetic over the wonders of Texas barbecue and the joys of Cajun/Creole cooking, that there is some good Mexican food to be found in San Antonio: "As the former capital city of the Mexican province of Tejas it was flamboyantly Spanish in architecture and manners, and today there is nearly a third of the city's population which is of Spanish or Mexican descent and loyal to their ancestral eating habits. Restaurants catering to this clientele go far beyond the usual Tex-Mex cuisine and offer authentic Mexican dishes not found elsewhere north of the Rio Grande. At sidewalk stands, women offer warm tortillas, tamales and tacos, while candy men, their trays on their heads, peddle sweets made of cactus, sweet potatoes, pecans, and sugar."

While El Cholo is the very heart and soul of the style of Mexican cooking that's become popular in Los Angeles, San Antonio can be said to be the birthplace of Mexican-American cuisine. It's home to the eating establishment that claims to be the oldest Mexican restaurant in America (though not always in the same location, as in the case of El Cholo). It's called the Original Mexican Restaurant, which from 1899 to 1960 sat at 117 Losoya Street, around the corner from the Alamo. (It's since moved across the river.) According to a curious little volume put out in 1950 by the Ford Motor Company called *The Ford Treasury of Favorite Recipes from Famous Eating Places*, the restaurant's most popular dish was its beef taco. In 1950, this was no doubt the very essence of exoticism. These days, it sounds rather quaint – the recipe even calls for ground beef boiled in water, which guarantees a nice pile of soggy hamburger. No wonder it's taken so long for Mexican cooking to earn the respect it deserves.

And thanks to the proliferation of fast food chains such as Taco Bell, a lot of Mexican cooking has gone from peasant food to fast food, without pausing in between as good food. Which reminds us of why, after seven decades, El Cholo shouldn't just be appreciated, it should be revered. This is a bastion of Mexican cooking as great cuisine. Not fine cuisine in the style of Classic French. But great cuisine in the style of Hong Kong seafood houses and Italian trattorias – cooking that can be appreciated for its goodness, without the attendant fuss of pretension and false formality. This is good chow for all of us.

Were I to boil down the cooking of Mexico, in general, and El Cholo and its Sonora Cafe, in particular, there would be three essential ingredients: the Three C's – Chiles, Chocolate and Corn. There's much more of course – this is a simplification in the extreme. But were you to remove any of those ingredients, Mexican cooking just wouldn't be Mexican anymore. The cuisine could exist without tequila, wheat or tomatoes. But it would crumble to dust without chiles, chocolate and corn.

A quick look at the menus at El Cholo and the Sonora Cafe does much to prove this point. The use of chiles abounds – the sweet *poblano* chiles in the remarkable Tortilla Soup, the textbook Chile Relleno, the chiles used to make the ubiquitous Pico de Gallo and the Honey-*Ancho* Chile Sauce that gives the vegetarian tacos such a kick. Corn is everywhere – from the corn tortillas to the green corn tamales to the smoked corn found in the Quesadilla *con Queso*. And chocolate is found in everything from the Mole Sauce to the Chocolate Praline Cake and White Chocolate Rice Pudding Tamales.

Chiles, chocolate and corn are ingredients of great antiquity in the cooking of Mexico. And so, for that matter, is much of the food consumed today. *Pozole*, the great hominy soup of Mexico, dates back at least a thousand years. *Pulque* (a milky alcoholic drink made from the fermented sap of various agaves) has been drunk for centuries. Bernardino de Sahagun, chronicler of Cortez's journey of conquest across Mexico, described meals of sweet tamales, turkey with tomatoes, squash seeds with chiles, tamales with beans, birds with dried corn, wild birds cooked with chiles and seeds. He also described far more types of chocolate than we know today. Half a millennium ago, Mexico was one of the best-fed lands in the world. And those ancient flavors are rife in the dishes found at El Cholo and the new generation of Sonora Cafe, the inheritor of uncountable centuries of culinary development.

·Chiles·

It would be tough to imagine the cooking at El Cholo and the Sonora Cafe without their rich blend of *poblano*, *pasilla*, *ancho* and *jalapeño* chiles. And it's their use of chiles that also reminds us of how very subtle the cooking at these restaurants can be. Rather than just tossing chiles into a recipe for the sake of having them – hot for the sake of hot – peppers are always integrated into the dishes with understatement. They're there, but they don't overwhelm. They're a spice in the stew, rather than the whole stew.

Chiles made their way north from Brazil and Peru, where South American primitives found them growing wild in the rainforest, and consumed them both raw and fire-charred as far back as 8,500 years ago. Within five thousand years or so, they'd traveled north to the land of the Aztecs, who received them as tribute from nations they'd conquered to the south. Tenochtitlan (now known to us as Mexico City) became a hotbed, as it were, of chile cultivation. And as their cultivation grew in sophistication, the variety of chiles grew in number, to the point where these days we're overwhelmed by the selection commonly available at Mexican markets – a mere fraction of the total number that exists.

Of the nondried chiles, there's the oft-mentioned chile *serra-*

no, usually found fresh or marinated in vinegar, a small, slim chile not much longer than two inches, colored a shade of green that's pleasing to the eye, with a flavor that's sharply picante, though not overly so. There's the chile *jalapeño*, larger and wider, with a texture less firm than the *serrano*, once again used both fresh and marinated in vinegar, with a flavor several levels more intense than that of the *serrano*.

There's the chile *poblano*, about twice the length of a *serrano*, much more intensely green, even dark in color, with a wide top, and a rumpled skin that tends to be wavy and dimpled. The *poblano* is known for a bend in its middle, and a flavor that's not so much picante as it is powerfully earthy. As a rule, it's roasted and peeled before use in the many stuffed chile recipes that call for the noble *poblano*. And there's the chile *guero*, which resembles the *jalapeño*, except it's a bit larger, and tends toward a yellow or yellow-green coloration, with a flavor that radiates heat throughout the mouth – a chile of considerable merit for those who like it hot. There's the Anaheim chile as well, mild but good for cooking. And the *habañero*, which is not so much Mexican as Caribbean, reputed to be the hottest chile in the world. And well it may be.

In the realm of the dried chiles, there's the ubiquitous chile *ancho*, which begins as a chile *poblano*, allowed to fully ripen, and then to dry, usually in the sun, into a dark brown color with a reddish tinge. There's the chile *mulato*, like the chile *ancho*, but darker still. The chile *pasilla*, even darker, a dried chile with a striking mouthful of heat. The chile *cascabel*, small, round and shiny. The chile *chipotle*, the trendy chile of the moment, in essence a *jalapeño* smoked and dried, which gives it an intensity of flavor that quite literally takes your breath away. The chile *pequin*, a favorite of the connoisseur of fiery flavors, is very small yet filled with enough potent heat to cause gasps of pleasurable pain. And there's the chile *arbol*, bright orange red; and the chile *guajillo*, light red and long like a string bean.

You'll find all manner of chile recipes in this book. Two of my personal favorites follow here.

EL CHOLO'S CLASSIC CHILE RELLENO

Serves 6

12 ounces aged grated cheddar cheese
6 whole canned *Ortega* chiles
6 eggs
12 ounces vegetable oil
1 teaspoon salt
Relleno Sauce (recipe below)

By hand, roll cheese into six football shaped balls of 2 ounces each. Wrap each ball in a chile. Put aside. Separate eggs, and beat whites in a bowl until they begin to stiffen. In a separate bowl, lightly beat the yolks. Fold yolks into whites. Preheat oil in frying pan. When hot, cook a small portion of the egg batter until it begins to set. Place *Ortega* chile on top, then pour on an equally small amount of batter to cover the chile. Turn and fry for two minutes more, until golden brown. Turn again, and continue to cook until golden brown all around. Place on plate, and top with 4 ounces of Relleno Sauce.

RELLENO SAUCE

1 tablespoon oil
3 medium garlic cloves (diced)
½ teaspoon Mexican oregano (dry)
½ medium yellow onion (chopped)
2 teaspoons white vinegar
1 medium green bell pepper (seeded and diced)
30 ounces canned whole peeled tomatoes in juice
2 whole Ortega chiles (peeled, seeded and diced)
2 teaspoons chicken base
1/4 teaspoon black pepper (ground)
2 whole bay leaves
salt to taste

In a large saucepan, heat the oil. Add the garlic, oregano, onion, vinegar, bell pepper and tomatoes. Bring to a boil and boil 2 minutes. Add the chicken base, black pepper, bay leaves and salt and let cook over low heat approximately 25 minutes. Remove from heat, discard bay leaves, and with a potato masher or wire whip, mash the tomatoes until sauce becomes chunky.

SONORA CAFE'S ANGEL HAIR PASTA WITH FRESH GULF SHRIMP, ROASTED PEPPERS AND *PASILLA* SAUCE

Pasilla chiles are also known as chiles *negros*, because of their intensely dark, brownish-red color. Like an *ancho*, they often have a wrinkled skin. But unlike an *ancho*, they have no trace of sweetness. The usually mundane angel hair pasta has never tasted better than when it's tossed with shrimp, peppers and *Pasilla* Sauce.

Serves 2

6 to 8 ounces fresh white angel hair pasta, cooked, drained
1 green bell pepper (roasted and peeled)
1 red bell pepper (roasted and peeled)
1 yellow bell pepper (roasted and peeled)
1 ounce virgin olive oil
12 large shrimp (peeled and deveined)
3 ounces garlic (finely chopped)
2 ounces shallots (finely chopped)
2 ounces unsalted butter
Pasilla Chile Sauce (recipe follows)
⅓ bunch cilantro (chopped)
4 ounces freshly grated Parmesan cheese
cilantro leaves and chopped parsley (garnish)

Roast the peppers on an open burner, turning constantly, until black all around. Place in a paper bag or food storage bag and steam about 20 minutes. Peel, remove ribs and seeds, cut peppers in half, then cut julienne.

Heat olive oil and sauté shrimp. Add garlic, shallots and butter and cook for 1 minute. Add 2 ounces of *Pasilla* Chile Sauce, chopped cilantro and roasted peppers. Mix well. Add pasta.

To serve, surround pasta with *Pasilla* Sauce sprinkled with Parmesan. Garnish with cilantro leaves and chopped parsley.

PASILLA CHILE SAUCE

Yields 2 quarts

6 dry *pasilla* chiles (*guajillo* chile optional)
1 ounce vegetable oil
4 garlic cloves (chopped)
½ yellow onion (chopped)
½ teaspoon whole oregano
½ teaspoon whole cumin
½ tablespoon whole black pepper
1 quart chicken stock
½ quart tomato puree
½ tablespoon chicken base
2 tablespoons roux (1 tablespoon butter, 1 tablespoon flour, cooked
    to golden brown)
salt to taste

Remove stems and seeds from chiles and be careful to wash hands after preparation to avoid burning eyes and skin.

To a pot of hot water, add chiles and simmer on very low heat 5 minutes. Strain and allow to cool, then blend. Heat oil in a high-sided pan, add garlic and cook to dark brown. Add onion and cook well for a few minutes. Add all spices and cook 1 minute. Add chicken stock, chile mixture, tomato puree and chicken base and simmer about 20 minutes. While hot, gradually stir in roux for thickness. Season to taste. Let simmer a few minutes, then strain sauce.

Chocolate

Though you won't find Mexican chocolate preparations like the Oaxacan wedding beverage called *chocolate atole* at El Cholo and Sonora Cafe, you will find such classic preparations as mole, and such modern creations as Salsa de Chocolate and White Chocolate Rice Pudding Tamales – flavors that do wonders when it comes to calming the palate after the fire of too much salsa.

The cocoa (or *cacao*) tree is native to Central America, the Caribbean and Mexico. And once again, it was used as a form of tribute from the conquered to the Aztecs, who wisely understood that gold was nice, but you can't eat gold. The chocolate was turned into a beverage – like water for chocolate – the recipe for which is still commonly used. You simply boil two cups of water in an *olla* (an earthenware pot) and add six ounces of Mexican chocolate, stirring until it's completely melted. Then, add two more cups of water, return to a boil, and beat with a *molinillo* (a whisk) until frothy. A blender will do as well, but a blender does not offer the flavor of time and antiquity.

In 1519, Hernando Cortez tasted chocolate prepared for him by the Aztecs at the court of Montezuma. An amanuensis in his entourage reported that he tasted chocolate in a paste as well, and a soup that was very possibly a version of mole, a dazzling Aztec creation of chiles and chocolate, two ingredients that seem destined never to meet in the same dish, yet which raise the flavor of chicken to a level rarely found in modern cooking.

EL CHOLO'S CLASSIC MOLE SAUCE
Yields 1 quart

¼ pound unsalted butter
¼ onion (peeled and chopped)
½ ounce garlic (chopped)
¼ cinnamon stick
¼ tablespoon whole allspice
½ bay leaf
2 whole cloves
¾ ounce *pasilla Negro* (stemmed, seeded and roasted)
¾ ounce *ancho* chiles (stemmed, seeded and roasted)
2 ¼ ounces Ibarra chocolate
4 ½ ounces pitted prunes
3 ounces raisins
1 ounce peanuts (toasted)
¼ ounce sesame seeds
1 ounce sliced almonds (toasted)
1 ounce pumpkin seeds (toasted)
¼ ripe plantain (peeled)
½ gallon chicken stock
½ ounce chicken base
1 ounce flour
½ ounce cornstarch

Melt butter in a sauté pan over medium heat. Add onion and garlic and cook until onion is soft. Add spices, chiles, chocolate, prunes, raisins, peanuts, sesame seeds, almonds, pumpkin seeds and plantain and continue to cook, stirring constantly, approximately 5 minutes. Then add chicken stock, chicken base and cook at medium heat 10 minutes, again stirring constantly. Then place mixture in a food processor or blender and puree. Return to medium heat. Mix the flour and cornstarch with water to make a paste. Add the mixture to the sauce as needed for desired consistency. Cook 5 minutes, stirring often, then strain.

White Chocolate Rice Pudding Tamales with Salsa de Chocolate

Serves 8

2 cups uncooked long-grain rice (or arborio)
1 ½ cups water
1 quart milk
2 cups half and half
2 14-ounce cans of sweetened condensed milk
1 cup sugar
1 teaspoon ground cinnamon
¾ cup raisins
1 cup grated white chocolate
15 corn husks (soaked in water at least 30 minutes)
Salsa de Chocolate (recipe follows)
fresh mint and powdered sugar for garnish

Hand-wash rice, draining water twice. Soak rice in water 2 hours or until water is absorbed. In a saucepan, add rice and rest of ingredients except white chocolate and cook slowly 2 ½ hours, stirring rice often with a wooden spoon. Remove from heat, stir thoroughly and let cool. Mix in the grated white chocolate.

Drain the corn husks and pat dry. Tear 6 1/4-inch strips from 1 husk for tying. Place 2 husks together with large ends overlapping by about 2 inches.

Spread about 6 ounces of the rice pudding mixture down the middle of the corn husk, leaving 1 inch at each end uncovered. Roll the corn husks so that the filling is completely enclosed (like a crepe). Twist and tie each end of the tamale with the 1/4- inch strips cut from the corn husk. Repeat the process for remaining tamales.

Place the tamales in a steamer set over gently boiling water and steam 5 to 7 minutes. Remove the tamales. Slice the tamales from end to end. Push the ends together as for baked potatoes. Pour some of the warm Salsa de Chocolate in center of a plate, placing a tamale over it. Garnish with mint leaves and powdered sugar, dusting the plate.

SALSA DE CHOCOLATE

Serves 8 (or 4 chocolate addicts)

1 tablet of Mexican chocolate (3 ounce)
¾ cup cream or evaporated milk (low-fat evaporated can be used)
pinch of cinnamon
3 tablespoons unsalted butter
¼ cup granulated sugar
¼ cup brown sugar
pinch (tiny) of cayenne pepper
⅓ cup unsweetened cocoa powder
2 teaspoons vanilla extract

Chop Mexican chocolate into small pieces. In a saucepan, place chocolate pieces, cream, cinnamon, butter, sugar, brown sugar, pepper, and cocoa powder. Heat on very low heat. When chocolate begins to melt, stir with a whisk. Heat about 5 more minutes until salsa is blended and smooth. Remove from heat and stir in vanilla. Serve over ice cream or brownies or both. This can be refrigerated, but when you reheat, add more milk or cream as the sauce will thicken up quite a bit.

·Corn·

If nothing else, the green corn tamale put El Cholo on the culinary map. It's been on the menu since 1927. And there are customers who have very likely eaten little else at El Cholo than the green corn tamale. It's a triumph of corn, the very essence of Mexican cooking at its best. And it's a reminder that without corn, Mexican food satisfies, but seems to cry out for its sweet *raison d'etre*.

Corn (better known as *maize*) was cultivated in Mexico around five thousand years ago (though wild kernels have been found in caves dating back nine thousand years), at about the same time as chiles and squash – making it a heck of a fine time to do some eating after several millennia of consuming dull mush, rocks and whatever small animals happened to wander by. By the time Columbus came upon the scene, there were more than 700 varieties of *maize* grown in Mexico and the surrounding lands. He brought some kernels back to Spain, where they were dubbed Indian corn, and grown for many years afterward as a novelty. In his writings, he described what he had found as, "a sort of grain which was well tasted, baked, dried and made into flour." As with many of his pronouncements, Columbus missed the point. Five centuries later, corn would have grown to be the second most commonly consumed grain in the world after rice.

So vital is corn to the history of Mexico and the West, that the *Encyclopaedia Britannica* has described it as, "the grain that built a hemisphere." In his book *Indians of the Americas* (quoted in Food by Waverley Root), John Collier writes that, "Without it, the Aztec, Mayan and Inca cultures and civilizations could not have come into existence."

By the time Cortez arrived in Mexico to destroy the Aztecs, *maize* tortillas and tamales were a standard part of the diet – not much different from their importance to the diet today. Waverley Root reports that, "Corn was so plentiful that it was planted along the road-sides so that those in want might help themselves, nobody in Mexico could die of hunger at a time when Europeans could and did." Interestingly, corn became a source of a multitude of joys – from the kernels themselves, eaten raw and prepared in any of a thousand ways, to the corn husks dried and turned into the wrappers for tamales, to the fungus that grows on corn called *huilacoche* – the truffle of Mexico.

"When the restaurant first opened, the tortillas were made by hand. Then, my grandparents started buying tortillas from a company called Ideal Tortilla that dates back to 1923. We still buy from them. We could buy tortillas for half the price, but their quality is still the best. We used to serve a plate of tortillas – hot, steamy tortillas between two plates with butter on the side. That was the traditional way. Now we serve chips, which are something the public forced on us. I wish we still served the hot tortillas, because I think it truly is a better dining experience. The tortillas were more important to us in those days because when you're eating just a straight tortilla, the quality is vital. And remember, in those days, we didn't have salsa that you dipped in. We had just a hot sauce and we put it in little tiny dressing bottles, almost like a honey jar, and you'd pour it on your tortillas. It was on the table all the time." – Ron Salisbury

EL CHOLO'S CORN TORTILLAS

Yields 24 tortillas

1 pound dried corn (either hominy, field or flint corn)
2 tablespoons powdered slaked lime (calcium hydroxide powder)
1 gallon water
1-1/4 cups warm water

Combine corn and lime in water, and steep over low flame for 10 to 12 hours, or until the corn is soft. Rinse the corn in cold water, then pulverize it in a food processor, or run it through a meat grinder, until the corn is finely ground. In a bowl, add about 1-1/4 cups warm water to the ground corn to form a thick masa – you want a dough that both holds together and is moist. You may have to keep experimenting till you get the texture right. The masa should form a ball. Divide the ball into 12 portions of about 2 ounces each. Flatten each ball using a tortilla press, or between the palms of your hands. Place on a hot *comal* or griddle, and cook for 1 to 2 minutes on each side.

SONORA CAFE'S BLUE CORN CHILE RELLENO

Blue corn is probably the most abused dish in Southwestern cooking, and the least understood. Indeed, it was the injudicious use of blue corn tortillas during the Southwestern cuisine fad of the eighties that may have shortened the cuisine's lifespan – many dishes were blue for the sake of being blue. In the case of this marvelous chile relleno, blue cornmeal is used as a dusting, giving the dish an imposing physical look without getting in the way of the flavors. And the relishes are a delight. Indeed, many diners find themselves ordering this dish not for the chile relleno itself, but for the easy-to-relish accompaniments.

Serves 6

6 *poblano* chiles (roasted and seeded, stems intact)
Cheese Mix (recipe follows)
Corn and Mushroom Relish (recipe follows)
flour for dusting chiles
6 eggs (whipped)
blue cornmeal to coat chiles
1 cup vegetable oil for frying
Avocado Salsa (recipe follows)

Roast the chiles, covering the stems with foil to protect them, and remove seeds. Stuff chiles with 2 ounces of Corn and Mushroom Relish and 2 ounces of Cheese Mix. Dust chiles with flour, quickly dip 1 chile at a time into the whipped eggs, then coat with the blue cornmeal. After all the chiles have been dipped and coated, heat 1 cup of oil to 325 or 350 degrees in a pan. Put 1 chile at a time in the pan and place a spoon on top of the chile to hold it down. Leave the chile in the oil no more than 1 minute. Remove chile from the oil and place in baking pan. Do not stack.

Preheat the oven to 400 degrees. Bake pan of chiles for 5 minutes. To serve, put 3 to 4 ounces of Avocado Salsa in the center of the plate and put the chile relleno on top of the salsa. Sprinkle some Cheese Mix over the relleno and serve the rest with the Corn and Mushroom Relish as side dishes.

CORN AND MUSHROOM RELISH

Yields 3 cups

2 *poblano* chiles (roasted, peeled, seeded and diced)
2 red bell peppers (roasted, peeled, seeded and diced)
4 tablespoons sweet butter
6 ears fresh sweet white corn (shucked, kernels cut off, about
    3 ½ cups)
1 cup wild mushrooms such as shiitakes, morels, golden
    chanterelles (cleaned and diced)
2 tablespoons cilantro (minced)
1 tablespoon marjoram (minced)
⅓ teaspoon white pepper
1 teaspoon *chipotle* chiles
1 teaspoon salt

Roast the chiles and peppers over an open flame, blistering the skins, turning frequently. Place in a paper bag or food storage bag and steam for about 20 minutes or until cool. Remove skins with your fingers or a knife and dice.

Heat a large heavy-bottomed skillet over high heat. Add the butter and corn and cook for about 3 to 4 minutes until the butter and corn get smoky and brown, tossing continuously. Add the mushrooms and remaining ingredients and cook for another 3 to 4 minutes until the mushrooms are thoroughly cooked.

CHEESE MIX

Yields 3 cups

8 ounces *manchego* cheese (grated)
8 ounces fontina cheese (cut into small squares or grated)
8 ounces mozzarella cheese (grated)

Mix all cheeses together in a medium bowl.

AVOCADO SALSA

Serves 4

2 medium-sized avocados (preferably Hass)
½ red bell pepper (stemmed, seeded and finely diced)
½ medium white onion (peeled and finely sliced)
1 tablespoon fresh cilantro (chopped)
1 ripe tomato (stemmed and finely diced)
1 *serrano* chile (stemmed, seeded and finely diced; be careful to
    wash hands after preparation to avoid burning eyes and skin)
juice of ⅓ lime
½ teaspoon kosher salt
pinch freshly ground black pepper

Cut the avocados in half, removing the pits, and cut into fine dice. Place in a bowl and fold in the remaining ingredients. Taste and correct the seasonings if necessary.

If you are not going to use this relish immediately, film top with olive oil and cover with plastic wrap. It will store at room temperature for an hour or two. Pour off the oil before serving.

CULINARY CULTS –
Nachos, Fajitas, Tamales and Margaritas

CULINARY CULTS

There are people who have gone to El Cholo for years, and have only tasted a fraction of the menu. Indeed, there are people so obsessed with a single dish, that's all they know of the restaurant. They've found perfection, and feel no need to go further. This is, of course, one of the secrets of any restaurant that lasts through the ages – a cult following of massive size. Philippe's the Original in downtown Los Angeles is fabled for its French dip sandwiches. Grey's Papaya in New York City is legend for its hot dogs. Pizzeria Gino in Chicago makes a pizza that brings tears to the eyes of true believers. Cafe du Monde in New Orleans has survived for many years serving nothing but beignet and coffee flavored with chicory. At El Cholo, cultists are quadruply blessed. Four items stand out as culinary objects of desire: the nachos, the fajitas, the green corn tamales and the margaritas. It's easy to get hooked on these delectables in the first place – even easier when they're as good as the versions available at El Cholo.

> "Our nachos came along thanks to a waitress named Carmen Rocha. She was originally from Texas, where nachos were born. You have to understand that at El Cholo, each waitress truly had her own room, which was her station, her own office. Guests would come on a regular basis every week to be served by Anne, or Carmen, or Beatrice, or whomever. Carmen started making nachos for her guests. And it caught on with other people in the restaurant. So we finally put them on the menu. We had never heard of nachos prior to that. And as far as I know, they were the first nachos in town." – Ron Salisbury

·Nachos·

It's the rare diner at El Cholo who doesn't ask for an order of nachos, a massive pile of tortilla chips, cheese, guacamole, salsa and *jalapeños* – the dish that for many *gringos* virtually defines Mexican cooking. Yet ask for nachos in Mexico City eateries, and you'll get a distinctly blank stare in return. They don't know about nachos at the *fondas* in the Plaza Garibaldi, they don't know about them at the superb Fonda El Refugio, they don't know about them in the Americanized coffee shop at the Camino Real Hotel. Nachos also don't appear in Diana Kennedy's definitive volume *The Cuisines of Mexico*, nor her *Tortilla Book*, nor her *Recipes from the Regional Cooks of Mexico*. But they do appear in *Los Angeles Times* writer Barbara Hansen's book *Mexican Cookery*, where they're simply corn chips topped with either melted Monterey Jack or Cheddar cheese, either *jalapeño* chilies or some good hot salsa (she also mentions refried beans and scallions as good alternative toppings).

Concerning the question of whether nachos have any Mexican roots at all, Hansen notes, "Nachos are one of those California slash Tex slash Mex things. The original was a very simple dish, just *jalapeños* and cheese and chips. Very simple. But they've glopped them up quite a bit. Nachos are to Mexican food what chop suey is to Chinese food – an American version that's been accepted as the real thing."

Those who believe in the dish's Mexican roots attribute its name and creation to Ignacio "Nacho" Anaya, a chef at the Victory Club in Piedras Negras, Mexico, back in the 1940s. As in the case of the Caesar salad and the Cobb salad, he allegedly ran low on food, and threw together most everything in his larder so that a group of women lunching at the club would have some snack food. He called it "Nacho's Special." A second claim of creation is by one Connie Alvarez King, who insists she concocted the first plate of nachos in 1943 at her restaurant in Harlingen, Texas, naming the snack after one of her workers, Ignacios, whose nickname was "Nacho."

It's worth noting that Los Angeles is very probably the nacho capital of the known world. Nachos are something more than ubiquitous in Los Angeles. They're burrowed so deep into the city's culinary consciousness that Angelenos no longer even perceive them as *ersatz* Mexican. They've become an American dish with a vaguely Spanish name. And the best in town, by a country mile, are the nachos served at El Cholo.

SONORA NACHOS

Serves 6

1 pound thick corn tortillas
vegetable oil as needed
Refried Beans (recipe on page 112)
1 cup shredded cheddar cheese
1 cup shredded Monterey Jack cheese
Relleno Sauce (recipe on page 29)
1 cup Guacamole (recipe on page 64)
1 cup sour cream

Cut each tortilla into sixths. Deep fry in oil until crispy. Drain on paper towel. Place on large ovenproof plate. Top with beans and cheeses. Place plate under broiler, to melt cheeses. To serve, drizzle with Relleno Sauce, top with dollops of Guacamole and sour cream.

··Fajitas··

Fajitas are a relatively recent arrival at El Cholo, having first appeared on the menu in 1984. That was the same year that most of America first heard the term *fajitas*. During the Republican National Convention in Dallas in 1984, it seemed as if every report emerging from Big D said something about how fajitas had been served at one grand and gala party after another, and how the delegates had all gone bonkers over the dish.

In almost no time banners proclaiming the presence of fajitas started appearing in front of Mexican restaurants all over Los Angeles. *Sunset Magazine* quickly jumped on the bandwagon, featuring the dish on its cover. And in nothing flat, fajitas spread from Mexican eateries to restaurants featuring California and American cuisines. It went from ethnic to nonethnic in almost nothing flat. When it hit, it hit big.

What exactly is the nature of the beast? Fajitas comes from the Spanish word *fajas*, meaning a "sash." Originally, the dish was made with skirt steak, the inner diaphragm muscle of a steer – the "sash" around the animal's midsection. Exactly where the dish began is, as ever, open to great quantities of dispute. One school of thought insists that fajitas were born and raised in San Antonio. And indeed, to this day, San Antonio is a major center of fajitas consumption. Others believe that fajitas are simply a modernization of the traditional Mexican grilled beef dish called *arrechera*, or that fajitas are a later evolution of a dish popular among the Indians who live in the desert around Sonora and Chihuahua. *Sunset* Magazine assumed the dish to have come from Mexican ranch hands working in the Southwest, who simply combined Mexican cooking styles with American ingredients (once again, shades of chop suey!). In a study conducted by Homero Recio at Texas A&M University, the source was determined to be the Roundup Restaurant in McAllen, Texas, where the dish was served under the name *botanzas*. Though it might also have originated at Sonny "Fajitas King" Falcon's food stand in Kyle, Texas. Or at Ninfa's Restaurant in Houston where it was called *tacos al carbon* (a dish carried at many restaurants, that's akin to, but not the same as, fajitas). Whatever the truth is (and usually it's many things – food evolves in a cyclical, not a linear fashion), fajitas are ubiquitous.

Beef is no longer the defining ingredient. Beef may have been the original fajitas ingredient, but chicken, shrimp and vegetables have been widely accepted (all four versions are available at El Cholo), along with Southern California oddities like lobster fajitas, moo shu fajitas, and potato skins filled with fajitas. The basic fajitas methodology involves strips of marinated steak, cooked in a heavy black iron skillet, with sliced onions and green peppers, served still sizzling with side orders of rice, beans, guacamole and tortillas. It all sounds so simple. It *is* simple – once you know the secrets. At El Cholo the secret is in the seasoning. Eating them at the restaurant is, of course, the ultimate treat, but it's also a visual feast, watching those clouds of fajitas smoke travel like locomotives through the restaurant.

CHICKEN FAJITAS

Serves 6 to 8

12 tablespoons vegetable oil
6 chicken breasts (skinned, boned and cut into thin strips)
6 green bell peppers (seeded and julienned)
6 red bell peppers (seeded and julienned)
4 red onions (peeled and julienned)
6 Roma tomatoes (julienned)
juice of 1 lime
Fajitas Seasoning, to taste (recipe follows)
8 tortillas, warmed
12 ounces mix of grated cheddar and Monterey Jack cheeses
sour cream
Guacamole (recipe on page 64)
Pico de Gallo (recipe follows)

In a large well-seasoned cast-iron or nonstick skillet, heat the oil and sauté the chicken, stirring well for about 2 minutes. When chicken is halfway cooked, add the peppers and onions and continue to cook for 2 minutes longer, stirring constantly. Add tomatoes and cook for 30 seconds. When cooked, add the lime juice and Fajitas Seasoning. Remove from heat and serve immediately with warm tortillas, cheese, sour cream, Guacamole and Pico de Gallo.

FAJITAS SEASONING

Yields about 2 cups

1/4 cup granulated garlic
1/4 cup Lawry's seasoned salt
1/8 cup chile powder
1/4 cup New Mexico chile powder
1/4 cup paprika
salt to taste
3 tablespoons ground cumin
3 tablespoons freshly ground black pepper
3 teaspoons ginger powder (optional)
3 teaspoons ground oregano

Combine all ingredients and store in a sealed container.

PICO DE GALLO

Yields 3 cups

5 roma tomatoes (finely diced)
1/2 medium yellow onion (finely chopped)
1/3 cup cilantro (finely chopped)
1 *guero* chile (seeded, stemmed, finely chopped; be careful to
    wash hands after preparation to avoid burning eyes and skin)
juice of 1 lime
salt and freshly ground pepper to taste

In a medium bowl, thoroughly mix all the ingredients except the lime juice, salt and pepper.

Add the lime juice and mix well. Season with salt and pepper and serve. Store in a sealed container.

·Tamales·

There's no dish that has the sheer obsessive following of the Green Corn Tamales at El Cholo. The flavor is, for the true believer, a little taste of heaven – a marvelous combination of corn and cornmeal, butter and cream, sugar and cheddar cheese, *Ortega* chiles, and corn husks to keep the whole thing together. At El Cholo, green corn tamales define summer every bit as much as a hot dog at Dodger Stadium. Families fight rush hour traffic to get to El Cholo for the season's first batch. People buy them by the dozen and take them home to freeze, so they can savor the melt-in-your-mouth creaminess year round.

All this devotion is curious for a dish that, until recently, has received little respect in the world of north-of-the-border Mexican cooking. Pity the poor tamale, the poor man of Mexican cooking, the traditional dish of the peasant, a dish so poorly regarded that at any number of Mexican restaurants they've been buried somewhere around the bottom of the menu, a poor relation to the seemingly more sophisticated enchilada, burrito and chile relleno.

Yet the tamale (actually, the singular should be *tamal*, but usage has rendered it tamale here in the United States) has a long and noble heritage – longer and nobler, in fact, than the enchilada, the burrito and the chile relleno. In her remarkable book, *The Cuisines of Mexico*,

Diana Kennedy begins her chapter on "Tamales and Tamal Dishes" by quoting from the *Historia General de las Cosas de Nueva Espana 1547-1582*, written by a conquistador named Sahagun, who describes how "They also ate many kinds of tamales, like pellets they are white and roundish, though not completely round nor exactly square . . . Other tamales are white and delicious as a fluffy, light biscuit . . . Another type are red, because after the dough is made, it's kept in the sun for two days, which burnishes it . . ." The green corn tamales at El Cholo are green gold, so burnished with goodness they virtually glow.

The more you learn about the tamale, the more amazing it becomes. Even more so than the American sandwich, this is a dish of unbelievable diversity and creativity. And yet, as with most of the wonderful dishes of the world, we're speaking here of a concoction of incredible simplicity – just meal, usually (but not always) made of corn, mixed with lard, filled with whatever, and wrapped in a leaf – usually (but not always) a corn husk. At its best, the tamale is a fine thing – a direct descendant of a dish eaten a thousand years ago by the Nahuatl Indians who gave the dish its name, and who knew that a house filled with billowing clouds of steam meant good tamales couldn't be very far behind.

"My grandparents came from Sonora, Mexico. But some of our recipes are from the Southwest. The green corn tamale recipe comes from Arizona, and was my grandmother's recipe. In her day, when there were bugs in the cobs or in the corn, nobody threw the corn away; they cut off the damaged part. Then, they'd cut away the remaining corn and make tamales with it, which was how the green corn tamales started."
– Ron Salisbury

GREEN CORN TAMALES

At El Cholo, the Green Corn Tamales are served only from May through October, because the corn is sweetest then. On *Cinco de Mayo* El Cholo sells out, despite the fact that the chef has made hundreds. One taste and you'll understand why.

Yields 12 tamales (8 ounces each)

24 ears yellow corn (best May through October)
½ pound cornmeal
¼ pound shortening
¼ pound unsalted butter
¾ cup sugar
½ cup half and half or cream
1 teaspoon salt
12 one-ounce strips of cheddar cheese
24-ounce can *Ortega* chiles
parchment paper, cut into squares
white cotton string

Cut both ends of the corn, remove the husks and save for wrapping. Cut the corn kernels off the cob. In a food processor, grind the kernels with the cornmeal. Set aside.

Beat the shortening and butter together until creamy. Add the sugar, half and half and salt. Add the corn mixture and mix well.

For each tamale, overlap two corn husks. Spread some of the corn mixture onto the husks. Place 1 cheese strip and 1 chile strip on top of the mixture. Top with more corn mixture. Bring the edges of the corn husks over the filling to cover completely. Place 1 husk on a square of parchment paper. Fold ends of corn husks up, over the tamale, then fold sides of parchment over tamale and fold up ends. Tie string around the little package to hold in place. Continue until all tamales are prepared.

Place on a rack and steam approximately 35 to 45 minutes.

"Margaritas"

It is clear to anyone who has ever tasted one, that the margarita served at El Cholo is the *crème de la crème*, the *sine qua non*, the best of the breed. For many people, El Cholo might as well be the restaurant where the margarita was born, although the first salt-rimmed delight wasn't served there until 1967. But so much tequila is used at El Cholo that it's the largest consumer of Cuervo 1800 tequila in the world. Even if it wasn't born there, it's where the margarita was raised to its highest level of being. Actually, it's not possible to point, with absolute certainty, to any one bar in the western world and say, without fear of contradiction, "It was here that the first margarita – the margarita primeval – was mixed, poured and then consumed." But there are many only too glad to take credit for this foamy drink of legendary potency.

One source says that the margarita was invented in 1936 by a bartender named Daniel Negrete, then manager of the Garci Crespo Hotel in Puebla, Mexico. Negrete, so the tale goes, had a girlfriend named Margarita Orozco, who was in the habit of licking a dollop of salt before taking a drink. So, to keep Margarita's hands out of the salt-cellar, Negrete created a drink with salt already laced around the rim. He would moisten the glass, dip it into the salt, then pour into it a mixture of tequila, Cointreau and the juice of the Mexican *limon*, shaken up with ice. The result: the margarita ... according to Daniel Negrete. (Nowadays, Negrete runs a bar in Ensenada called El Grande Chapparal. He has a patent for the margarita from the Mexican government, and he'll gladly show it to anyone who asks.)

It would be convenient to believe that the margarita began in the hands of Daniel Negrete in a bar in Puebla. But there are those who disagree, fiercely. Also claiming to be the birthplace of the margarita is the old Tail o' the Cock that sat for many years on La Cienega Boulevard in Los Angeles. The Tail o' the Cock margarita was supposedly invented by a fellow named Johnny Durletter in the early fifties, in honor of a young, but never identified, starlet who frequented the restaurant. The popularity of the drink at the Tail is said to have led an American tequila importer to sponsor a national advertising campaign using the slogan: "Margarita – More Than a Girl's Name."

Yet another genesis of the drink is offered in *The Tequila Book*, in which the authors Marion Gorman and Felipe De Alba quote one Teddy Stauffer (described as "Mr. Acapulco") as claiming that: "Popular, vivacious Margarita Sames has been coming to Acapulco with her rancher husband for over twenty-five years. They had a house near the Flamingo Hotel and gave lots of parties. She loves tequila and drinks all day long. She would go into a bar and ask them to mix her some tequila with Cointreau and *limon*, and serve it in a cocktail glass. I know Margarita very well, and that has always been her drink. She claims she was the first to make it a drink."

To add to the confusion, *The Tequila Book* also credits the margarita to Dona Bertha, owner and bartender of Bertita's Bar in Taxco, Mexico, back around 1930. Dona Bertha had already created a drink she called "Bertha," so naturally the next drink she invented she called "Margarita." And, as a final fillip, the Agua Caliente Race Track in Tijuana proudly states that the margarita was invented in its clubhouse bar.

The recipe for the margarita is the one cult recipe that isn't offered in this book. Families are entitled to their secret recipes, aren't they? As is noted in the chapter on the history of El Cholo, the recipe is a closely kept secret, jealously guarded, never shared. Spies have hung out at the bar to uncover that secret. They've offered bartenders bribes and rewards. Barflies have tried to woo the recipe away. But all to no avail. Whatever the secret is, it makes the margarita at El Cholo the best – tart and sweet at the same time with a bright tequila undertone, and the ability to make you feel as if you've left your body. Beware – the secret seems to make it remarkably potent as well. And lest good cooks learn to make every recipe in this book as well as the chefs at El

Cholo, there remains one very important reason to visit the restaurant whenever in Los Angeles: The margarita is superb.

In lieu of the world's best margarita recipe, I offer the one I use at home. Let us just call it the world's second-best.

"My dad never wanted hard liquor, so it was always beer and wine. We only served wine with dinner – a red Claret from Italian Swiss Colony and a white Sauterne – in little juice glasses. When I purchased the restaurant from my dad in 1966, I realized we had to shift with the times and there was a growing need for margaritas. I didn't know anything about cocktails at that point. I didn't even drink. So we opened up a bar and started as best we could.

"A very quiet man named Emil Smith used to dine here. Always ate by himself. In those days I used to be at the register and when he'd come to pay I'd always ask, "How was your dinner tonight?" One night, he said, "Fine as usual, but your margaritas are terrible. Would you like me to show you how to make a good margarita?" I accepted his invitation. He owned a little restaurant in a strip mall – a typical steak and martini and scotch place. He shared the recipe for margaritas. That's how we ended up with our margarita recipe. Who knows how many years it would have been if it hadn't been for him. At times I think maybe I want to make it a little tarter, so I'll remove a little bit of the sweetening agent, and the whole thing goes off balance. There's a chemistry that exists between all the ingredients. If you change the balance, everything goes haywire. We have seven different ingredients that go into the El Cholo margarita and the chemistry can't be trifled with. Only five or six people actually know the recipe – our chefs, myself, and my sons." – Ron Salisbury

THE WORLD'S SECOND-BEST MARGARITA

juice of half a lime
½ ounce of Triple Sec
1 ounce of Cuervo 1800 Tequila
coarse salt to rim the glass

Chill champagne glasses. Just before serving, dip the rim of the glass into a mound of coarse salt to coat it. In a shaker, shake all ingredients with ice cubes. Strain into the salt-rimmed champagne glass. Serve immediately.

FROM EL CHOLO'S KITCHEN

FROM EL CHOLO'S KITCHEN

The very essence of the cooking at El Cholo is simplicity. And yet, it's a simplicity that's deceptive. For even though many of the recipes seem basic, they're the results of years (and in some cases centuries) of trial and error. Many of the dishes on the menu at El Cholo have roots that stretch back into the mists of history, back to the cooking of the ancient Aztecs and Mayans, as they embarked on a journey of culinary serendipity: discovering that tomatoes were more edible when red than when green, for instance, or that certain peppers are hotter than others, or that with some simple processing the bitterness of chocolate could be turned sweet. What El Cholo's food provides are flavors, especially the complex levels of flavors in the sauces and salsas, which have been found to blend and mesh to a degree that can be almost astonishing. This is cooking that can be savored on any number of levels. To the casual diner, the dishes at El Cholo taste just plain good – there's such simple satisfaction in an order of guacamole, nachos, tamales, enchiladas. But for those who spend the time letting the flavors roll over their tongues, subtle complexities emerge. They can appreciate the way, for instance, that in the basic hot sauce, the flavor of the whole tomatoes differs from the sweet astringency of the tomato puree, the crunch of the diced yellow onions differs from the soft sourness of the green onions. In the case of El Cholo, a hot sauce isn't just a hot sauce; it's a gift from the ages, handed down to us by generations of great Mexican cooks. In its balance, in its layers, in its contrasts, it's the perfect hot sauce. And it makes you thirst for a good swallow of Mexican beer to boot.

Every recipe included here has been tested by time and by Chefs Roberto Juarez and Felix Salcedo, the fine chefs in charge of the cuisine that has made El Cholo's food a legend. Don't be afraid to reduce, double, triple, even quadruple the measurements, depending on the size of the group you are serving. The only caution is to slowly and carefully increase the amount of salt to avoid an overly salty dish.

FLOUR TORTILLAS

Yields 12 tortillas

8 ounces butter
12 ounces hot vegetable oil
1 teaspoon salt
1-½ pounds flour
16 ounces warm milk

Place butter, oil and salt in food processor or mixer. Quickly combine. Add flour. With the processor or mixer operating at slow speed, add the warm milk, mixing for about 5 minutes at the slowest speed. Turn to next higher speed, and mix for 5 minutes. Then, turn speed up one more notch, and mix for another 10 minutes. The object is to create a consistency that's soft yet thick. Remove dough, and begin to make 3-ounce balls by hand. Place on a metal sheet or tray, and let stand for 10 minutes. Then, using a wooden roller, start stretching the dough (use your fingers to make the stretching easier). Place on a hot *comal* or griddle, and cook for 1 to 2 minutes on each side.

"Gary Cooper used to come in his yellow Duesenberg and he always liked strawberry jam with his flour tortillas. When we knew he was coming, someone would have to run up to the grocery store and buy a bottle of strawberry jam so Gary Cooper could have his strawberry jam with his flour tortillas. Since that time, we have never had anybody who has asked for strawberry jam with flour tortillas." – Ron Salisbury

TACOS AL CARBON

Very probably the best known, and best loved, of all Mexican dishes, the taco is so prevalent north of the border that it's difficult to think of it as being a Mexican dish at all. The term *al carbon* refers simply to shreds of charcoal-grilled meat. It's a sandwich, pure and simple, rich with flavor, served with tortillas that are fried (hard) or warm and moist (soft). The taco at El Cholo is the Platonic essence of the dish – served with plenty of condiments to make it your own.

Serves 4

1 green bell pepper (roasted, peeled, seeded and sliced)
1 red bell pepper (roasted, peeled, seeded and sliced)
1 yellow bell pepper (roasted, peeled, seeded and sliced)
2 pounds top sirloin
2 pounds bacon
8 flour tortillas
8 ounces Monterey Jack cheese
Cooked Tomatillo Sauce (recipe follows)

Roast the peppers over an open flame, turning frequently, blackening the skin. Place in a paper bag or in a food storage bag and steam 20 minutes or until cool. Peel the skin off with your fingers, remove the seeds and ribs and slice.

Cook the top sirloin on a grill. Cook each side 2 minutes, then cut into strips. Fry the bacon, then chop it.

Put 2 tortillas on a plate, add cheese and grilled sirloin, bacon, bell peppers, Hot Sauce and Cooked Tomatillo Sauce.

COOKED TOMATILLO SAUCE

Yields 1 quart

1 quart water
4 cups tomatillos (husked and cut)
1 teaspoon fresh garlic
1 small onion
2 *jalapeño* chiles
salt to taste
white pepper

In a medium pot combine all ingredients except salt and pepper and bring to a boil. Boil for 15 minutes. When cooked, pour into a blender and puree. Cook over low heat for 5 more minutes and season with salt and white pepper to taste.

"In time we had to take into consideration that the environmental experience was becoming very important in dining. We had to stay true to our history, but at the same time provide a more interesting setting. Roslyn Smith redesigned the original El Cholo, and then the other restaurants in their entirety. She was the only designer who looked at El Cholo, looked at those old walls, and wanted to preserve them, to enhance the original feeling. She gave us a plan. I owe so much to her. Everything you see at the Santa Monica branch is her influence. She says she walks into an empty space, and she sees everything, the signs, the colors, everything." – Ron Salisbury

GUACAMOLE

Serves 6

5 ripe avocados (preferably Hass)
½ ripe tomato (finely chopped)
1 ½ yellow hot chiles (finely chopped)
1 ½ *Ortega* chiles (finely chopped)
1/8 bunch cilantro (finely chopped)
1 teaspoon fresh lemon juice
¼ teaspoon salt
¼ yellow onion (finely chopped)

In a large bowl, mix all the ingredients together with a wire whip or a potato masher. Mash until mixed well and desired consistency is reached.

"Guacamole is another item that all of a sudden just showed up. For years, we never added anything to the menu. It was the same menu year after year. If you look at the original menu, there were just the combination plates, a tostada and chili con carne. There were no chimichangas or burritos. In 1955 my uncle Jimmy said, 'I'm going to introduce something new here.' And he made guacamole. I can remember the first day. Everybody went wild over it. To this day, I don't think anything equals the taste of our freshly made guacamole." – Ron Salisbury

HOT SAUCE

If Mexican cooking was a religion, its bible might read: "In the beginning, there was the sauce." In this case, a hot sauce of fine and elegant proportions, nicely balancing the sweet acidity of tomatoes with the sharp fire of the chiles, a sonata that increases in intensity as onions (yellow and green) are added, modified with cilantro, raised to a fine art with oregano and garlic. Make lots – it goes well on a multitude of dishes. But for tacos it's a must.

Serves 16 (about 6 ounces each)

1 60-ounce can whole peeled tomatoes, drained
3 cups tomato puree
7 yellow hot chiles
½ bunch cilantro
½ yellow onion (diced)
1 tablespoon garlic (chopped)
2 whole green onions (chopped)
3 cups water
1 tablespoon Mexican oregano (dry)
2 teaspoons freshly ground black pepper
salt to taste

In a food processor or a blender, blend the tomatoes, adding the tomato puree. Transfer tomato mixture to a bowl. In the food processor or blender, blend the chiles, cilantro, onion, garlic, green onions, adding the water, oregano and black pepper. Once blended, add the chile mixture to the blended tomatoes and mix with a wire whip, adding salt to taste.

CHEESE ENCHILADAS

Somewhat oddly, some guides refer to the enchilada as a Spanish-American dish, whose name supposedly is a portmanteau that translates loosely as "filled with chili." A dish, according to these guides, that's more for tourists than for locals. This is curious, for enchiladas are found on virtually every menu in Mexico, and seem to have originated in both Puebla and Oaxaca, where they're eaten by much of the population. If this is a tourist dish, then Mexico is a land where everyone is a tourist. And El Cholo is definitely a restaurant where everyone is a tourist, for it's the rare diner here who doesn't order an enchilada – some occasionally, and some very single time. The El Cholo enchilada is definitive – firm yet yielding, multilayered, multitextured, and, of course, multipleasured.

Serves 6

½ cup vegetable shortening
6 corn tortillas
12 ounces shredded Monterey Jack cheese
12 ounces grated aged cheddar cheese
Enchilada Sauce (recipe follows)
3 ounces yellow onion, finely chopped
3 ounces green onion, chopped

Pour oil into heavy skillet until the bottom is well covered, then heat until oil begins to smoke. Cook tortillas one at a time until they begin to brown on each side, but are still soft. On an ovenproof plate, top each tortilla with a generous helping of cheese, roll up and arrange in a heated serving dish with the seam facing down. When dish is full, top with Enchilada Sauce and remaining cheese, and bake at 350 degrees until cheese is melted. Garnish with onions.

ENCHILADA SAUCE

8 ounces California chiles, dried
8 ounces *pasilla* chiles, dried
½ small can tomato puree
1 teaspoon cumin
1 teaspoon black pepper
1 ½ teaspoons allspice
1 teaspoon Mexican oregano, dried
1 teaspoon beef base
1 ½ teaspoons salt
1 teaspoon Kitchen Bouquet
1 quart water
1 tablespoon flour
2 tablespoons shortening

Combine all ingredients, except for flour and shortening. Boil 1 1/2 hours. During the last 15 minutes, combine flour and shortening into a roux, and add slowly to sauce as it boils, until it thickens. Cook over medium heat for another 45 minutes. Remove from heat and strain.

"My El Cholo story began twenty-five years ago. My mother and father were dining at El Cholo. My mother was eight-and-a-half months pregnant with me. When I started to smell El Cholo's wonderful aromas . . . I just had to get out to try some of the nachos, tacos and fajitas. My parents rushed to the hospital, and I was born. They had to leave their meals half eaten. This is the only time anyone in my family has left a meal half eaten at El Cholo." – Lee Ernesto Recinos

SONORA ENCHILADA

Call it an enchilada on steroids – this one has everything. The sweet spice of red sauce, the haunting backbite of green sauce, a filling of richly flavored chicken stew, a topping of Monterey Jack cheese, red onions, eggs, olives and sour cream. It's a big enchilada (perhaps the Whole Enchilada), with a different combination of flavors in every bite. As the centerpiece of a Mexican feast, it works just fine. And it's ever so easy to make.

Serves 6

18 corn tortillas
vegetable oil as needed
4 cups Red Sauce (recipe follows)
3 cups canned black beans
4 cups shredded Monterey Jack cheese
4 cups Sonora Enchilada Chicken Filling (recipe follows)
4 cups Green Sauce (recipe follows)
6 eggs
1 cup sliced black olives
½ cup red bell pepper, chopped
1 cup sour cream

Preheat frying pan over medium heat. Heat vegetable oil. Dip tortillas in hot oil, quickly cooking on both sides without allowing tortillas to become crisp. Continue until all are fried, adding oil as necessary. Dip 1 tortilla per person in Red Sauce and place on a large ovenproof plate. Top with 1/4 cup black beans and a sprinkling of the shredded Monterey Jack cheese. Dip a second tortilla into the Red Sauce. Place it on top of the first tortilla. Top with 1/2 cup of chicken filling. Liberally top 1 side of the top tortilla with Red Sauce and one side with Green Sauce. Sprinkle generously with shredded Monterey Jack cheese and red onion. Heat under a broiler (or in a 350 degree oven) until cheese is well melted. While cheese is melting, fry 1 egg per enchilada. Top final product with fried egg, a sprinkling of olives, chopped red pepper and a dollop of sour cream.

RED SAUCE

1 teaspoon fresh garlic, chopped
6 *guajillo* chiles, dried
4 California chiles, dried
3 *arbol* chiles, dried
1 medium yellow onion, chopped
1 quart water
vegetable oil as needed
salt to taste
1 teaspoon coarsely ground black pepper

In a medium pot, combine all ingredients except salt, pepper and oil. Bring mixture to a boil, and cook for 15 minutes over high heat. Pour into a blender or food processor, and puree ingredients. Preheat oil in saucepan. Add puree, salt and pepper. Cook for 5 minutes. Strain.

SONORA ENCHILADA CHICKEN FILLING

2 cups cooked chicken, shredded
1 tomatoes, chopped
1 fresh *pasilla* chile, chopped
1 green bell pepper, chopped
1 teaspoon Mexican oregano, dry
1 teaspoon white ground pepper
1 clove garlic, finely chopped
1 tablespoon salt
1 quart water

In a saucepan, combine all ingredients, cooking over medium heat. Bring to a boil and cook for 30 minutes, or until a soft texture is achieved.

GREEN SAUCE

1 quart chicken stock
1 medium onion, chopped
3 whole, fresh *jalapeño* chiles
3 green bell peppers, chopped
2 bunches of spinach
1 pound tomatillos, husked
salt to taste
1 teaspoon ground white pepper
vegetable oil as needed

In a medium pot, bring chicken stock to a boil. Add remaining ingredients except for salt, pepper and oil. Bring to a boil, cook 15 minutes over high heat. Puree in blender or food processor. Heat oil in saucepan, add puree, salt and pepper, and cook for 5 minutes. Strain.

"I had just arrived in Los Angeles from New York, when a close friend asked if I'd like to meet the fabulous Michelle Phillips on a blind date at a one-of-a-kind Mexican restaurant. A hard-bitten New Yorker, I was unsure of how I felt about Mexican food (there being no great south-of-the-border restaurants in the Big Apple). But I was sure of how I felt about meeting Ms. Phillips. I was treated to a *muy especial* margarita, and a heavenly dish of melted cheese called nachos. It was green corn season, so my dinner companions insisted I try the tamales. Perhaps it was the new city. But I'm more inclined to think it was the company who made me realize this was the best meal of my life." – Geoffrey Tozer

ENCHILADA SUIZA

Despite what you might expect, the enchilada *Suiza* (Swiss enchilada) does not get its name from Swiss cheese. Instead, its name seems to come from the richness of its filling, a rich chicken stew that, in some versions, is made with heavy cream. (The chefs at El Cholo have lightened up their rendition a bit.) It's an excellent enchilada for people who don't want to deal with lots of hot sauce and intense flavors.

Serves 6

6 corn tortillas
4 ounces vegetable oil
2 cups shredded Monterey Jack cheese
Enchilada Suiza Chicken Filling (recipe follows)
Enchilada Suiza Tomatillo Sauce (recipe follows)
1 cup sour cream
1 cup mixed red and green bell peppers, chopped

Preheat oil in frying pan. Fry each tortilla in hot oil, cooking on both sides, being sure that tortilla does not become crisp. On each of six ovenproof plates, place 1 tortilla. Top with a little more than 1/4 cup of shredded Monterey Jack and 3 ounces of chicken filling. Roll closed, using a toothpick (if necessary) to maintain integrity and shape. Top with more shredded Monterey Jack and Tomatillo Sauce. Heat under broiler (or in 350 degree oven) until cheese is well melted. Garnish with sour cream and chopped bell pepper mix.

"It was 1950, my junior prom. I had just enough money to cover a wrist corsage, gas for my 1937 Ford, and dinner for two at El Cholo. Alas, my date ordered dessert (the great flan, great even then!), which took us over budget. But the waiters took great pity on my sweating tuxedo – and said it was on the house!!" – John Orloff

ENCHILADA SUIZA CHICKEN FILLING

2 whole boneless chicken breasts
3 ounces vegetable oil
1 green bell pepper, roasted and sliced
1 red bell pepper, roasted and sliced
1 yellow bell pepper, roasted and sliced
1 cup heavy cream
ground white pepper and salt to taste

Preheat oil in frying pan. Over medium heat, sauté chicken breasts, adding more oil as needed. Cook for four minutes on each side, then cut into two inch slices. In a medium pot, place chicken slices and add remaining ingredients. Cook over low heat for 15 minutes.

(Note: To roast peppers, place over open flame, supporting peppers on the end of a fork, turning until the skin of the pepper is blackened. Peel, remove seeds and stems, slice. Wash hands carefully after handling peppers to avoid irritation to skin and eyes.)

ENCHILADA SUIZA TOMATILLO SAUCE

1 quart chicken stock
1 medium yellow onion, chopped
2 fresh *jalapeño* chiles
3 green bell peppers, chopped,
2 bunches spinach
1 pound tomatillos, husked
vegetable oil as needed
salt to taste
1 teaspoon ground white pepper

In a medium pot, combine all ingredients except for oil, salt, and pepper. Bring to a boil, cook for 15 minutes over high heat. Once cooked, puree in blender or food processor. Heat oil in saucepan, cook puree for five minutes, salt and pepper to taste. Strain.

CRABMEAT ENCHILADA WITH JALAPEÑO-CILANTRO PESTO SAUCE

There's a wealth of crab (*jaiba*) in the Gulf of Mexico, but crabmeat has traditionally been merely a footnote ingredient in Mexican cooking, found mostly in the distinctive dishes of Veracruz – spicy crab soup (*chilpachole de jaiba*) and stuffed crab (*jaibas rellenas*). Crab is perceived, and rightly so, as a special-occasion dish. And that's what this preparation from the Sonora Cafe is – a dish to be served to the most special of guests, using the best crabmeat available, flavored with a *Jalapeño*-Pesto Sauce. It's a dazzling creation – new yet traditional at the same time.

Serves 6

4 ounces butter
6 ounces white wine
12 mushrooms, chopped
1 cup onions, chopped
1 pound Dungeness crab, shredded or chunked
½ bunch cilantro, chopped
salt to taste
1 teaspoon white pepper
6 corn tortillas
2 cups aged Monterey Jack cheese, grated
Jalapeño-Cilantro Pesto Sauce (recipe follows)
Crabmeat Sauce (recipe follows)
½ cup sour cream
1 avocado, sliced
slices of lime

In a saucepan, melt butter in white wine over medium heat. Add mushrooms and onions. Cook for three minutes. Add crabmeat, cilantro, salt and pepper. Cook for ten minutes more over low heat.

Preheat oil in frying pan over medium heat. Fry tortillas in hot oil, quickly cooking both sides until warmed but not crisp. On an oven-proof plate, place 1 tortilla. Top generously with Monterey Jack cheese and crabmeat mixture. Roll closed, holding in place with toothpicks, if necessary. Top half the tortilla roll with Jalapeño-Cilantro Pesto Sauce, and half with Crabmeat Sauce, finishing with a further layer of Monterey Jack. Heat under broiler (or in 350 degree oven) until cheese is melted. Garnish with sour cream, avocado and lime.

JALAPEÑO-CILANTRO PESTO SAUCE

2 bunches cilantro, chopped
¾ teaspoon garlic, chopped
1 tablespoon pine nuts
2 fresh *jalapeños*, chopped
1 cup water
1 ½ limes
1 ½ teaspoon salt
3 ounces vegetable oil

In a blender, add all ingredients except for oil. Blend until a paste-like texture is achieved. Then, slowly drip in oil as if making a mayonnaise.

CRABMEAT SAUCE

6 ounces butter
3 garlic cloves, chopped
1 shallot, chopped
6 ounces white wine
1 cup whipping cream
1 teaspoon salt
1 teaspoon ground white pepper
2 teaspoons cornstarch
4 ounces milk

In a medium-sized saucepan, melt the butter. Add the garlic and shallots, and cook until softened. Add white wine, cooked until reduced. Add cream, salt and pepper. In a separate bowl, mix cornstarch and milk until smooth, then add to thicken the garlic mixture.

VEGETARIAN ENCHILADA

There are few cuisines more vegetarian-friendly than Mexican. All those beans! All that rice! That corn! The hungry vegetarian, weary of brown rice and millet, can get lost in the joy of enchiladas made with a rich palette of vegetables. Almost any vegetables work here; this is a dish limited only by the creativity of the cook.

Serves 6.

Julienned Vegetables (recipe follows)
2 ounces butter
salt to taste
6 corn tortillas
2 cups grated Monterey Jack cheese
Corn Cream Sauce (recipe follows)
Tomato Sauce (recipe follows)
3 green onions, chopped
1/2 cup chopped pecans

In a pan, sauté julienned vegetables in butter until soft yet crunchy and salt to taste. On each of 6 ovenproof plates, place one corn tortilla. Top generously with Monterey Jack cheese and Julienned Vegetables. Roll closed, holding in place with toothpicks if necessary. Top the tortilla roll with about 3 ounces of the Corn Cream Sauce, finishing with a further layer of Monterey Jack. Heat under broiler (or in 350 degree oven) until cheese is well melted. Garnish with Tomato Sauce, green onions and pecans.

> "If you were here throughout our first fifty years, you'd remember that the walls didn't have pictures or any colors. The walls were old and when my dad and mom opened in 1931, the walls were white. But over the years, the cigarette smoke and general aging made the walls very dark. There was a charm, an old charm." – Ron Salisbury

JULIENNED VEGETABLES

8 ounces sweet butter
2 bunches spinach, blanched and strained
1 large peeled carrot, julienned
1 large green zucchini, julienned
1 whole yellow bell pepper, julienned
1 whole green bell pepper, julienned
1 whole red bell pepper, julienned
2 ears sweet corn, shucked and cleaned
12 button mushrooms, sliced
1 cup grated Monterey Jack cheese
1 cup grated Mozzarella cheese
salt to taste

In a preheated frying pan, melt butter. Add all vegetables and sauté for four minutes, turning often. Salt to taste.

CORN CREAM SAUCE

1 ounce unsalted butter
1 small yellow onion (diced)
3 garlic cloves (chopped)
½ quart heavy cream
½ quart half and half
¼ teaspoon white pepper
1 teaspoon sugar
salt to taste
16 ounces canned yellow corn

Melt the butter in a large saucepan over low heat. Add onion and garlic and sauté approximately 2 minutes. Add the cream, half and half and white pepper. Bring to a boil and boil 15 minutes. Add sugar, salt and corn. Cook for 2 minutes to heat corn. Remove from heat and blend.

TOMATO SAUCE

1 ounce olive oil
2 garlic cloves, peeled and minced
1/4 red onion, peeled and cut into 1/4 inch dice
1 Anaheim chile, roasted, peeled and seeded
1 teaspoon fresh cilantro, finely chopped
1/4 teaspoon ground black pepper
1/4 teaspoon ground cumin
1/4 teaspoon dried Mexican oregano
1/4 teaspoon whole thyme
4 Roma tomatoes, cored and diced
4 ounces tomato juice
salt to taste

In a medium sauté pan, heat olive oil over medium heat. Add garlic and sauté until brown. Add onion and continue browning for 2 to 3 minutes. Add chile, cilantro and other herbs and spices. Sauté 8 to 10 minutes. Add tomatoes, and cook 10 more minutes, stirring to prevent sticking. Add tomato juice, bring to a slow boil. Add salt to taste. Cool and strain.

"My husband first took me to El Cholo when we started dating. It became a weekly outing for us. We always sat at 'our' table, on the porch, next to the fountain. Every week, we'd make a wish. We got married and continued our ritual at El Cholo – ending each meal, hand in hand, throwing our coins in the fountain. Not knowing if I would be able to bear a child, we each knew what the other was wishing. But we never said a word. When I finally found out, I wanted the moment to be extra special for my husband. We went to El Cholo, sat at our favorite table, and ended our meal in the usual way. Only this time, I said my wish out loud, 'Now, I wish for a healthy baby.' My husband looked at me with tears in his eyes, and we both threw our coins in the fountain." – Patricia Murphy

CHICKEN TAMALES

The word comes from the Nahuatl *tamalli*, and the variations approach the infinite. Some Modern Southwestern chefs are so obsessed with tamales, they produce dozens of variations – we've even encountered variations filled with caviar. In Mexico, the tamale is traditionally a dish of celebration, often served at Sunday dinner, and at feasts like All Saints' Day. In Merida and Oaxaca, they're usually wrapped in banana leaves, while corn husks are used in the rest of the country. There are tamales on the menu all year round at El Cholo. One of the great pleasures of the El Cholo tamale is how devoid of gimmicks it is – it's a tamale, pure and simple, and ever so good.

Makes 24 tamales

**2 to 3 bunches of corn husks, washed and soaked in hot water
   overnight, drained and patted dry
Tamale Masa (recipe follows)
Tamale Sauce with Chicken Filling (recipe follows)**

Lay two corn husks flat. so that they overlap. Spread a spoonful of Tamale Masa mixture lengthwise over the center of the husks, leaving bare husk at the top, bottom and sides for wrapping. Spread a spoonful of Tamale Sauce with Chicken Filling over the dough. Fold both sides of the husk inward, so that they overlap. Fold the ends towards the center, so that they overlap. Tie the tamale with a strip of corn husk or string.

Fill the bottom of a steamer with water, dropping in a clean coin (it will rattle if the steamer goes dry). Line the bottom of the steamer with corn husks. Place the tamales upright in the steamer, packing them in firmly, but leaving room for the dough to swell as the tamales cook. Cover with a layer of corn husks, and top with a clean cloth to absorb condensed moisture from the lid of the steamer. If needed, add more boiling water during the cooking process. Keep the steamer lid on tight. Steam the tamales for 1 hour. To test if they're done, remove one, and check to see if the dough comes away easily from the husk. If so, they're done.

TAMALE MASA

2 1/4 pounds fresh corn masa or prepared masa flour
1 1/2 cups water (boiling the water with 30 tomatillo husks will
    make the dough fluffier)
1 1/4 teaspoons baking powder
1/2 cup cornstarch or rice flour
1 1/2 to 2 tablespoons salt
1 pound lard or shortening

    Place fresh masa or prepared masa flour in a large bowl. Add water gradually and knead until smooth and no longer sticky. Add baking powder, cornstarch and salt to taste. (Steaming will slightly reduce the saltiness of the dough.) In a separate bowl, beat the lard or shortening by hand, or with an electric mixer until it's fluffy, about five minutes. Work the lard into the masa, kneading thoroughly until the mixture is smooth. (Test to see if it's light enough by dropping a bit into a glass of cold water. If it floats, it's light enough. If not, keep kneading.)

TAMALE SAUCE WITH CHICKEN FILLING

6 cups water
6 ripe tomatoes
1-1/2 medium white onions, peeled and quartered
5 garlic cloves
4 fresh whole *jalapeños*
1/2 cup vegetable oil or soft lard
salt and pepper to taste
Chicken Tamale Filling (recipe follows)

    In a large saucepan, bring the water to a boil. Add tomatoes, onions, garlic and *jalapeños*. Simmer for 25 minutes. Cool, then puree in a blender or food processor. Heat the oil or lard in a heavy saucepan, add the pureed mixture, cook until thick. Add salt and pepper to taste. Add the cooked chicken to the tamale sauce, and cook at a medium temperature for ten minutes.

CHICKEN TAMALE FILLING

3 1/2 quarts water
1 whole chicken, cut into pieces
2 leeks with most of the green tops
1/2 head garlic, peeled
3 whole cloves
3 black peppercorns
1 sprig fresh cilantro
salt to taste

In a stockpot, bring water to a boil. Add chicken, and all remaining ingredients. Simmer 45 minutes, or until chicken is tender. Remove from heat, allow chicken to cool in the broth. Remove chicken from broth and shred into large pieces. Reserve broth.

"My father and I have a tremendous adversarial relationship. He graduated from UCLA, so I graduated from USC. He likes British cars and I drive a Porsche. The list goes, but the theme is the same – we do things differently for competitive reasons and not rational ones. This situation made it nearly impossible for my father, who is on the board of directors of the Physician's Food and Wine Society, to agree that El Cholo was great, if only because it was my recommendation to have lunch there. But he did seem to really enjoy the food, though he was guarded and reluctant to reveal his opinion. The afternoon flew by and it was time for dinner. I could not believe it when he said that we would have dinner at El Cholo. I had triumphed! With all the great food in L.A., the connoisseur chose El Cholo." – John Campbell

HOLIDAY TAMALE

In Mexico and throughout the Southwest, holidays are never simply spiritual occasions. They're special times of the year celebrated with food. And more food. And more food. And what better food with which to celebrate than the modest tamale, raised to the level of haute cuisine, a grand and glorious holiday dish worth dreaming of all year round.

Serves 18

3 pounds banana leaves (cut into 10 x 10 inch squares), available in most Latin markets. About 40 corn husks can be substituted if banana leaves are unavailable.
Masa for Holiday Tamales (recipe follows)
3 pounds cooked and shredded turkey or chicken breast
Apple Compote (recipe follows)
3 cups Mole Sauce (recipe follows)

Heat the banana leaves over an open flame for a few seconds just to make them easier to handle. Spread about 4 ounces of prepared masa almost to the edges of the leaf, making a thin layer. Mix the turkey or chicken with the Apple Compote. Place about 1 tablespoon of this mixture in the middle of the masa, forming a nice thick line. Fold the side edges of the leaf lengthwise over the filling, overlapping in the center. Fold the top and bottom ends toward the center, overlapping, and tie with long strips of banana leaves.

To steam, arrange tamales upright in a prepared steamer. Place lid on steamer and steam 1 hour at medium to low heat. When masa no longer sticks to the banana leaf, tamales are done.

Serve with the Mole Sauce.

MASA FOR HOLIDAY TAMALES

2 ¾ cups vegetable shortening
5 ½ pounds masa
1 ½ tablepoons baking powder
2 ¼ cups sugar
kernels from 15 ears of corn
9 tablespoons salt
3 tablespoons white pepper
9 tablespoons vanilla extract
4 tablespoons ground cinnamon

In a mixer with a wire whip attachment, mix the shortening until fluffy. Remove whip, attach paddle. Mix the masa, baking powder and sugar and very gradually add mixture to the shortening. Add the corn and mix well. Add salt, pepper, vanilla extract and cinnamon and mix well 5 minutes. Place masa in a bowl.

APPLE COMPOTE

8 ounces butter
pinch of ground cinnamon
pinch of ground nutmeg
pinch of ground cloves
4 ounces brown sugar
4 ounces water
4 apples (peeled, cored and diced)
4 ripe plantains (peeled and diced)
1 cup raisins
1 cup pitted prunes (sliced)

Melt butter in a heavy-duty pot over medium heat. Add spices and brown sugar and cook until caramelized. Add water and cook 2 minutes. Add apples, plantains, raisins and prunes and cook over low heat 10 minutes, stirring constantly.

BURRITO DORADO

The word *dorado* literally means "gilded." And when a dish is wildly gilded with flavors like this burrito is, it's blessed with the honorific. Some years ago, I came across a dish called "won ton *dorado con salsa escabeche*" that was so astonishingly flavorful, that I ate three orders in a row. The Burrito *Dorado* is worthy of the same homage. Like the fabled golden city of El Dorado, it's a treasure – in this case one that's very easy to find.

Serves 6

6 large flour tortillas
24 ounces Refried Beans (recipe on page 86)
24 ounces Spanish Rice (recipe on page 87)
24 ounces Chile Con Carne (recipe follows)
12 ounces grated aged cheddar cheese
12 ounces grated aged Monterey Jack cheese
6 whole canned *Ortega* chiles
24 ounces Relleno Sauce (recipe on page 29)
12 ounces Guacamole (recipe on page 64)
12 ounces sour cream

On each of 6 ovenproof plates, place 1 large flour tortilla. Top generously with about 4 ounces each of Refried Beans, Spanish Rice and Chile Con Carne. Fold closed. Mix cheeses. Cut *Ortega* chiles in half. Top burrito with Relleno Sauce, 2 halves of an *Ortega* chile, relleno sauce, and a thick sprinkling of both cheeses. Heat under broiler until cheese is melted. Serve with Guacamole and sour cream on the side.

BURRITO DORADO CHILE CON CARNE

Serves 6

2 1/2 pounds beef chuck
1 1/2 quarts water
2 teaspoons salt
16 ounces tomato puree
1 teaspoon ground cumin
1 teaspoon coarsely ground black pepper
1 teaspoon dried oregano
1 teaspoon Lawry's seasoning salt
1 cup beef stock
1 teaspoon garlic, chopped
1 teaspoon Kitchen Bouquet

In a large pot, simmer beef in water and salt for about 1 1/2 hours. When tender, refrigerate, remove fat, then cut into cubes. Return to pot with remaining ingredients. Simmer about 1 hour or until tender.

"In the late forties, when we were starving students at UCLA, the big event was dinner at El Cholo. The delicious guacamole dinner for two. The guacamole in the tortilla cups in the center of the plate, a slice of olive on top, surrounded by a chile relleno, a cheese enchilada, beans with thin spaghetti or rice. All this for $1.20 each." – Donald and Margaret Fenton

BEEF BURRITO

In its most basic form, the burrito is a large taco, made out of a thin, soft tortilla that's been folded closed. The tortilla can be of flour or corn. The burrito itself can contain beans or not, meat or not, cheese or not, salsa or not. It falls under the general heading of *antojitos Mexicanos*, "little cravings" or "little whims," of which the burrito is often the most whimsical. As served at *antojito* stands, it's very possibly the single heaviest fast-food item in the world, with each often weighing in excess of a pound. The name supposedly means "little burro" – and that little burro can carry some serious weight.

Serves 12

3 pounds good-quality beef
1 cup corn or safflower oil
8 *ancho* chiles, roasted and seeded
8 garlic cloves
½ onion, chopped
salt
12 corn tortillas

Cut the beef into long thin strips. In skillet, heat half the oil until it begins to smoke. Brown the meat on both sides. Place the cooked meat in a stew pot, cover with water, and boil until tender, about 2 hours. Cool and shred with a fork.

In a blender, puree the chiles, 2 of the garlic cloves and the onion. Add water as needed.

In a heavy skillet, heat half the remaining oil. Crush the remaining garlic cloves, and add to the oil. When they begin to brown, add the shredded beef, stirring until well cooked. Add the chili puree. Cook until well blended. Remove from skillet. In the remaining oil, heat the tortillas, fill with meat mixture, roll closed and serve. If you wish, Spanish rice and refried beans can also be added.

REFRIED BEANS

A misnomer that's come to be accepted as proper terminology, deriving from the term *frijoles refritos*, which translates as "well-fried beans," not "refried beans." As the recipe indicates, they're not refried at all. That's unless you have leftovers the next day, of course, at which time you can fry them and they taste just great. There's almost nothing that can be done to ruin this most basic of basic dishes.

Serves 6

2 cups dry pinto beans
10 cups water
2 tablespoon salt
4 ounces vegetable oil, heated
4 ounces aged grated cheddar cheese and Monterey Jack

In a one-gallon pot, add beans, water and salt. Cook over high heat for 1 1/2 hours, until beans are tender. Reduce water to a minimal amount. Add hot vegetable oil and both cheeses. Using a potato masher, mash until consistency is thick and rich.

"Ah, those tostadas and combo plates – Jose, the head chef, really knew his business. And those beautiful and beautifully dressed waitresses. Talk about job satisfaction – in honor of their years of service, various dining rooms bore their names, and the room's festive decor added the master stroke that made dining at El Cholo a unique treat. Today, our grandchildren are El Cholo fans, making three generations of our family lovers of good Mexican food. *Viva* El Cholo!" – John Maxwell

SPANISH RICE

Like Brussels sprouts and French fries, Spanish rice is little known in the land for which it's named. It's a pleasant reminder of the days when Mexican food was referred to as Spanish cooking. And for those who grew up on Spanish rice in cans (many of us did), the difference in flavor is the near side of remarkable. Canned corn may be acceptable, but canned rice is an abomination.

Serves 12

1 ½ ounces oil or vegetable shortening
1 yellow onion (diced)
2 garlic cloves (finely chopped)
2 quarts water
2 green bell peppers (seeded and diced)
2 16-ounce cans of whole peeled tomatoes or crushed tomatoes, drained
1 ½ tablespoons chicken base
1 teaspoon salt
4 cups long-grain white rice

In a large saucepan, heat the oil. Add the onion and garlic and sauté 1 minute. Then add the water, bell peppers, tomatoes and chicken base and let boil about 10 minutes, then add the salt. Lower the heat and continue boiling 5 minutes until the peppers and onion are soft. Add the rice and keep stirring 2 minutes. Cover the pot, lower the heat and keep covered until broth becomes absorbed, about 15 minutes.

TOSTADA COMPUESTA

A tostada could be described as a fried tortilla. But that would be missing the point. For like the noble sandwich, the tostada can be topped with myriad ingredients, which are "glued" to the tortilla surface with a coating of refried beans. The basic tostada *compuesta* is a fine starting point; from there, the construct, like a Dagwood Sandwich, is up to you.

Serves 6

6 ounces vegetable oil
6 large corn tortillas or 10-inch flour tortillas
3 cups refried beans
6 tablespoons chorizo
3 cups dried Monterey Jack and grated aged cheddar cheese, mixed
18 ounces lettuce (shredded)
2 cups beets (diced)
2 cups jicama (sliced)
2 cups carrots (sliced)
2 cups red cabbage (sliced)
2 cups green beans
2 cups green peas
6 tomato wedges (for garnish)
1 cup dried Monterey Jack cheese (for garnish)
1 bunch watercress (for garnish)

Preheat frying pan. Heat oil. Fry tortillas one by one, two minutes on each side, until crisp. Place each fried tortilla on its own plate. Add beans, chorizo and cheese. Layer lettuce and vegetables on top.
Garnish with tomatoes, cheese and watercress.

CARNITAS

The word means "little meats," a culinary understatement that translates into one of the most meltingly delicious ingredients in Mexican cooking – pork long-simmered in massive pots, with all of the fat rendered out (the equivalent of the Eastern European dish, chicken *gribenes*), so that the remaining meat is astonishing in its crunchiness. In Mexico, the pieces of pork are often served still attached to the skin, as a *chicharron*.

Serves 6

5 pounds pork shoulder, cut into six 12- to 16-ounce chunks
4 cups vegetable oil
1 tablespoon salt
¼ teaspoon black pepper
1 tablespoon garlic (chopped)
2 bay leaves (crumbled)
4 ounces of cola soda
½ cup milk
flour tortillas
garnishes of lime, avocado wedges, rings of red onion

Trim as much fat and gristle as possible from the pork. Heat the vegetable oil in a deep covered skillet to a temperature of 200 degrees.

Mix together the salt, pepper, garlic, and bay leaves. Coat pork pieces completely with mixture, shaking them to remove any excess. Add the pork to the heated vegetable oil and sear to brown on all sides. Reduce the heat to the barest possible simmer and cook the pork 1 hour, turning every 20 minutes. Add cola and milk to pork and continue cooking 30 minutes more.

Drain the pork on paper towels, then place on a platter and garnish with lime, wedges of avocado and onion rings. Serve with flour tortillas.

CHIMICHANGAS

The chimichanga was born in the north of Mexico, in the state of Sonora, though most people connect it with Arizona. And for good reason – it's the rare restaurant in Arizona that doesn't serve chimis in one form or another. The dish is basically a deep-fried burrito stuffed (in this case) with chicken, though just about anything else will do – from *picadillo* to *chorizo*, from pork *carnitas* to turkey. As long as it crunches, it's a fine chimichanga.

Serves 4

1 pound shredded cooked chicken
4 flour tortillas (medium)
4 toothpicks
6 cups vegetable oil for deep frying
shredded lettuce
Guacamole (see recipe, page 64)
1 ounce tomatoes (diced)
1 ounce onion (diced)
8 ounces cheddar cheese

Place a scoop of the chicken in the center of a tortilla and roll it like an eggroll, tucking in the ends. Secure with toothpicks and repeat with the remaining tortillas.

Heat the oil to 375 degrees in a deep heavy pan and add the rolls with tongs, not crowding them in the oil. Fry until golden brown and drain on paper towels.

To serve, place on bed of lettuce with Guacamole, tomatoes, onion, and cheese.

GUAJILLO SAUCE

Guajillo is not a mild chile. One of the most delicious, intense of the dried chiles, it's long and narrow in shape, a lighter red than many other chiles, with a smooth skin and a surprisingly sharp chile bite. A smaller variety is called *pulla*, which proves that hot things come in small packages – it's even hotter than the *guajillo* – and brave folks can subsitute it here.

Serves 10 (about 5 ounces each)

4 ½ ounces oil or vegetable shortening
½ yellow onion (diced)
5 garlic cloves (chopped)
8 dried *guajillo* chiles with seeds
1 teaspoon ground or whole cumin
½ teaspoon freshly ground black pepper
8 cups water
1 tablespoon chicken base
½ cup flour
2 teaspoons salt

In a large saucepan, heat 2 1/2 ounces of oil approximately 4 minutes. Add the onion and garlic and sauté 3 minutes until onion is translucent. Add the chiles, cumin, black pepper and sauté 1 minute. Lower the heat, add the water and chicken base. Bring to a boil and boil 10 minutes. Remove from heat and blend mixture in a blender or food processor. Set aside.

Meanwhile, in a 10-inch sauté pan over low heat, add the remaining 2 ounces of oil. When oil is hot, slowly whisk in the flour and keep whisking approximately 5 minutes or until the flour is brown. Remove from heat.

Pour the chile mixture into a saucepan, bring to a boil and boil 5 minutes. Lower the heat, add the flour mixture and boil 5 minutes. Add the salt, remove from heat and strain through a strainer.

SEAFOOD SOFT TACOS

Very much a dish for the nineties – the soft taco, surrounding the culinarily correct tenderness of scallops, shrimp and sea bass. It's a dish, in other words, that tastes good, and is good for you.

Serves 4

½ pound fresh scallops
½ pound Mexican shrimp (peeled and deveined)
½ pound fresh Mexican sea bass (trimmed and cut into pieces)
salt and pepper
¼ cup salad oil
½ pound jicama (cleaned, peeled, cut into julienne strips)
½ pound chayote squash (cleaned, peeled, cut into julienne strips)
1 carrot (cleaned, peeled, cut into julienne strips)
1 yellow zucchini (cleaned, peeled, cut into julienne strips)
1 small red bell pepper (stemmed, seeded, cut into julienne strips)
1 small green bell pepper (stemmed, seeded, cut into julienne strips)
4 ounces medium mushrooms (cleaned and sliced)
¼ bunch of cilantro (washed and chopped)
salt and pepper to taste
8 flour tortillas (cut into 5-inch diameter)
Cooked Tomatillo Sauce (see recipe, page 63)

Mix seafood with salt and pepper and marinate in oil up to 1 day. Sear seafood with a little oil in a hot skillet just before assembling. Reserve marinade.

Lightly toss vegetables with mushrooms and cilantro in a medium bowl. Pour a little of the marinade into a sauté pan over high heat, add vegetables and sauté about 3 to 4 minutes. Add salt and pepper and return vegetables to bowl.

To warm tortillas, bring a *comal* or medium sauté pan to medium-high heat. "Burn off" each tortilla on both sides in the pan, cooking it just until a few black spots appear. Place tortillas on a warm platter and cover with plastic wrap until ready to serve.

To serve, put 2 double tortillas on a 10-inch plate. Place 1 shrimp, 1 scallop and 1 piece of fish on each tortilla. Add about 1 ounce of Tomatillo Salsa on top of fish, then top with the vegetable mixture and fold taco-style or serve open-face.

SEAFOOD ENCHILADAS

Seafood enchiladas are a whole meal, a feast of serious proportions, redolent of oregano and cumin, napped with rice and beans, as fine a plate as you'll find anywhere on the Pacific Coast of Mexico, made all the better with fish fresh-caught in local waters.

Serves 4

1 *poblano* chile (roasted, peeled, stemmed and seeded)
2 *serrano* chiles (stems removed)
10 fresh tomatillos (husked and washed)
2 cups chicken broth
1 teaspoon fresh cilantro (chopped)
2 tablespoons olive oil
½ cup onion (chopped)
2 cloves garlic (minced)
½ pound firm white fish (cooked and shredded)
½ red bell pepper (stemmed and seeded, chopped)
1 cup diced tomato
1 tablespoon fresh Mexican oregano (chopped)
½ teaspoon ground cumin
vegetable oil for frying
8 tortillas
8 ounces Monterey Jack cheese (shredded)

Roast the chiles over an open flame, turning constantly, until the skin is black all around. Place in a paper bag or food storage bag and steam 20 minutes. Peel with your fingers, remove seeds and stem and cut. To make the sauce, place the chiles, tomatillos, broth and cilantro in a blender or food processor and puree until smooth. To make the filling, heat 2 tablespoons oil in a skillet and sauté the onion and garlic until soft. Add the fish and continue to sauté until browned. Stir in the bell pepper, tomato, oregano and cumin and cook 5 minutes or until thickened. To assemble, heat the oil in a skillet and dip each tortilla in the oil until softened, about 3 seconds per side. Place some of the fish filling on the tortilla along with a little cheese, then roll up. Place in a baking pan. Repeat with the remaining tortillas. Top with some of the sauce and bake in a 350 degree oven until heated through and the cheese melts, about 10 minutes. Garnish with additional cheese and serve.

ORIGINAL CHILE CON CARNE

Though no longer on the menu at El Cholo, the chile survives here as a heritage dish. A taste of the original menu from 1927, when chile was one of the most popular items at the restaurant, and perceived as a bit exotic to boot – a taste of how times have changed, as has the spelling. Today we know it as "chili."

Serves 4

4 pounds chuck roll (cut into cubes)
2 cups water
2 tablespoons salt
2 bay leaves
2 cups tomato puree
1 teaspoon cumin
1 teaspoon black pepper
1 teaspoon oregano
1 teaspoon garlic
1 tablespoon allspice
4 *pasilla* chiles (dry)
4 California chiles (dry)

Put meat, water, salt and bay leaves in a pot and cook for 45 minutes. When meat is soft, add all other ingredients, lower the heat and continue cooking 30 minutes. Add salt to taste.

"My sister and I came all the way from Philadelphia to eat at El Cholo. We had the best tacos from the other side of the Mississippi. We will return." – Tyler and Ashton Sildue

SOPA SECA DE FIDEO (DRY VERMICELLI SOUP)

The term is a bit odd, for *sopa seca* translates as "dry soup," an oxymoron if there ever was one. What it turns out to mean is starch cooked in broth, be it pasta, rice or tortillas. In this case, the starch is the Mexican vermicelli called fideo. On feast days, by the way, there are usually two soups – first a "wet" one (*sopa aguada*) followed by a dry one (*sopa seca*). As the folks at Campbell's like to say, soup is good food.

Serves 6

6 tablespoons peanut or safflower oil
8 ounces fine vermicelli in bundles
1 ¼ pounds fresh tomatoes or 2 ½ cups canned, drained (coarsely
    chopped)
¼ small onion (coarsely chopped)
1 clove garlic (peeled and coarsely chopped)
½ cup chicken broth or ½ cup water plus 2 chicken bouillon cubes
2 whole *chipotle* chiles (dried or canned Heroez)
sea salt (or regular) to taste
¾ cup sour cream or *crème fraîche*
2 or 3 ounces grated Chihuahua cheese or mild cheddar

Preheat the oven to 350 degrees. Grease a small casserole or glass loaf pan.

Heat the oil until it smokes, then lower the flame a little and fry the bundles of vermicelli until they are a deep golden brown. They brown quickly, so turn them over from time to time. Do not break up the bundles. Remove from the oil.

Blend the tomatoes with the onion and garlic until smooth. Add to the oil in the pan and fry over high heat, stirring well from time to time, about 8 minutes. Add the broth, chiles and salt, and cook 3 minutes longer. Add the fried pasta to the tomato sauce. Stir well, then cover the pan and cook over a rather low flame until all the liquid has been absorbed, about 8 to 10 minutes.

Transfer pasta to the prepared pan. Spread the sour cream over the top, sprinkle with the cheese, and cook 20 to 30 minutes, or until the pasta is just coming away from the sides of the dish and the cheese is well melted.

TORTILLA SOUP

Like a lot of dishes that are, these days, considered to be rather fine, tortilla soup began as a way of making a dish more filling using a filler that might otherwise be tossed away. Like Tuscan bread soup, tortilla soup uses chips and strips (both stale and otherwise) as a thickener in the soup. In the Southwest, it's a dish found at just about every diner and greasy spoon. At El Cholo and the Sonora Cafe, it's been turned into an almost elegant creation – a dish that isn't so much filler as a clever meal-in-a-bowl.

Serves 10

3 tablespoons olive oil
1 whole white or yellow onion (diced)
2 tablespoons garlic (minced)
3 whole red bell peppers (diced and seeded)
1 tablespoon whole cumin
1 quart chicken stock
1 tablespoon chicken base
1 quart fresh tomato puree (12 to 15 blanched, peeled tomatoes)
1 quart canned tomato puree
1 bunch fresh cilantro (chopped)
4 bay leaves
2 tablespoons Tabasco sauce
1 tablespoon Mexican oregano
1 tablespoon coarsely ground black pepper
1 tablespoon whole fresh thyme
1 6- to 8-inch branch of fresh rosemary
4 tablespoons finely minced *chipotle* chiles (salsa *jalapeño* is an adequate substitute)
2 tablespoons sugar
1 teaspoon salt
4 corn tortillas
1 bunch cilantro
1 large onion (diced)
4 boneless, skinless breasts of chicken
4 whole *pasilla* or *poblano* chiles
2 whole avocados
4 ounces feta cheese (aged dry jack, jack or cheddar may be used)

In a large heavy skillet, heat olive oil and sauté the first 4 ingredients until the onions and peppers are tender, but not brown.

While sautéing, in a large soup pot, combine the next 14 ingredients. Heat to a boil and lower to simmer. Add the sautéed contents and continue to simmer about 1 ½ hours.

At this point, one of two things may be done. If a thick soup is desired, remove the rosemary branch and bay leaves and puree soup in a blender. If a thinner soup is desired, strain through a cheesecloth.

While the soup is simmering, prepare the garnishes that will be added to each bowl of soup just before serving. Slice corn tortillas into thin julienne strips and deep fry until crisp; drain thoroughly. Wash, drain, and pick over cilantro. Coarsely chop cilantro if desired. Sauté large diced onion until golden brown. Broil or grill chicken breasts until golden brown and cut into julienne strips. Roast chiles directly on top of stove burners until skins crackle and are black. Scrape off skins and remove stems and seeds, cut into julienne strips. Dice two ripe avocados and set aside in a bowl of cold water just enough to cover and the juice of 1 lemon. Grate, crumble or shave the cheese of your choice.

Place soup in individual bowls, garnish with diced chicken, cheese, chiles, cilantro, avocado and tortilla strips.

"Corn tortillas have been my mainstay since I was a child. We needed no menus; Mom knew what we wanted – a plate of rice and beans to go along with the steaming hot corn tortillas. All I ever asked for were more tortillas and butter – *please*! The tradition has carried on now that I am married. In fact, my new family tradition began at El Cholo. One night in May of 1989 I found my diamond engagement ring hidden in a plate of corn tortillas." – Shannon Stowell Cisneros

Albondigas Soup

Pity the poor *albondiga*, a wonderful meatball turned to rubber by virtually every chef who touches it. Except in this case, where the texture is perfect, the flavors complex, the dish irresistible. It's said to cure what ails you as well – call this Mexican chicken soup, but made with beef, of course.

Serves 6

6 tomatoes (skinned and diced)
1 onion (diced)
1 green bell pepper (diced)
1 teaspoon fresh garlic (chopped)
salt and pepper to taste
1 gallon fresh chicken stock
1 pound ground beef
1 egg
1 tablespoon flour
1 piece of *Ortega* chile (finely chopped)
1 tomato (finely chopped)
¼ bunch green onions (finely chopped)
1 teaspoon cumin
1 teaspoon black pepper
1 teaspoon chopped fresh cilantro
1 teaspoon chopped fresh mint
salt if needed
cilantro for garnish

Combine first six ingredients in a stockpot over high heat. Bring to a rolling boil. Lower the heat and simmer 20 minutes. Mix next 11 ingredients in a large bowl. Place 1 gallon of cool water in a large pot. Make 24 small meatballs and add them to the pot. Bring to a boil and boil 20 to 25 minutes. Let meatballs cool, then add to soup. Serve soup in individual bowls with meatballs and garnish with cilantro.

Sopaipillas

The most cheerful of desserts, a happily puffed-up pillow, a deep-fried fritter sweetened with honey, cinnamon and/or powdered sugar, a perfect sweet at the end of a meal filled with spice. In the El Cholo rendition, surprisingly light, though best if served very hot and fresh – *sopaipillas* seem to increase logarithmically in density as they cool. Interestingly, though this dessert appears in Mexico, it's best known in New Mexico, possibly having originated in Albuquerque, where its more rounded cousin is called a *buñuelo*.

Yields 16 *sopaipillas*

1 cup all-purpose bleached flour
2 teaspoons baking powder
1 teaspoon salt
1 tablespoon sugar
1 tablespoon vegetable shortening
⅓ cup hot water
1 or 2 tablespoons flour, if needed
peanut oil for frying
powdered sugar
honey

Put first 5 ingredients in a mixing bowl. Use fingers or a pastry blender to thoroughly combine and evenly distribute shortening.

Add hot water and stir with a fork until mixture forms a dough. If dough is too dry to mold or knead, add a bit more water. If dough seems too wet, add 1 to 2 tablespoons flour. Knead a couple of times, then place in a plastic bag and let rise 1 hour in a warm place.

Lightly flour a work surface and roll dough into a rectangle about ¼ to ⅓ inch thick. If the dough seems too elastic to roll easily, cover and let rest a few minutes more, then roll again. Fold the dough in half and roll the rectangle again. Cut the dough into 3 x 4-inch rectangles.

Heat at least 5 inches of oil in a 3-quart saucepan or deep-fryer to 350 to 360 degrees. Fry 1 or 2 at a time, spooning hot oil over the top to encourage puffing. Drain on paper towels. Immediately dust with powdered sugar and serve with honey.

WARM CHOCOLATE CAKE WITH IBARRA CHOCOLATE SAUCE

Forget the sweet pile called Death by Chocolate found at restaurants from coast to coast. The true essence of a chocolate overdose is this wholly indulgent chocolate cake with its powerful coffee kick, and its alluring topping. One bite goes a long way. And one bite is never enough.

Serves 10

12 ounces semisweet chocolate (chopped)
¼ cup Frangelica liqueur
¼ cup freshly brewed strong coffee
1 cup heavy whipping cream
5 large eggs
⅓ cup sugar
Ibarra Chocolate Sauce (recipe follows)
vanilla ice cream

Preheat the oven to 350 degrees. Butter and flour a 10-inch round cake pan. In the top of a double boiler over barely simmering water, melt the chocolate and set aside. In a medium saucepan, heat the Frangelica and coffee. Add the melted chocolate and do not stir. Set aside at room temperature.

In the bowl of an electric mixer, whip the cream until stiff peaks form. Cover and refrigerate until needed. In a stainless steel bowl that is set over a saucepan of hot water, whisk the eggs and sugar until warm. Remove from the saucepan and with an electric mixer, whip the eggs and sugar until soft peaks form and the mixture has tripled in volume. Mix 1/4 of the whipped egg-sugar mixture into the chocolate mixture. Fold the chocolate mixture back into the remaining egg-sugar mixture. Fold in the whipped cream until blended.

Pour the batter into the prepared cake pan. Place the pan in a larger pan of warm water that comes halfway up the sides of the cake pan, and bake 30 to 40 minutes or until the cake has risen and small cracks appear on the surface. Let cool 15 to 20 minutes, top with Ibarra Chocolate Sauce and serve with vanilla ice cream.

To reheat, preheat the oven to 300 degrees, cover the cake

loosely with foil and place in the oven with heat turned off. Let warm about 10 minutes.

IBARRA CHOCOLATE SAUCE

2 eggs (separated)
½ cup sugar
1 tablespoon Ibarra chocolate
1 cup heavy cream

In a mixing bowl, beat the egg yolks and sugar together and set aside. Melt the chocolate in a bowl over simmering water. Bring the cream to a boil and pour half of the mixture into the egg mixture slowly to temper the eggs. Beating vigorously, put the remaining cream mixture in the pan back over the heat. Slowly pour the tempered egg mixture into the saucepan and whisk vigorously while adding the chocolate. Cook until the mixture smoothly coats the back of a spoon, about 3 minutes, whisking constantly. Strain and cool slightly.

SONORA CAFE

FROM SONORA CAFE'S KITCHEN

FROM SONORA CAFE'S KITCHEN

Six decades after El Cholo was born, Ron Salisbury decided to take the venerable cooking of their 1927 institution and meld it with the new cuisine of modern Southwestern chefs such as Stephen Pyles, Dean Fearing, Robert Del Grande, Mark Miller. The result, thanks to Executive Chef Felix Salcedo, was Sonora Cafe, which spent its first years in downtown Los Angeles before moving to its present location on La Brea Avenue, a street filled with art galleries and trendy shops. The result is a restaurant as creative as El Cholo is traditional, an eatery where the only borders are those of taste – if it tastes good, there's a fine chance Chef Salcedo will try it.

CAESAR SALAD

Serves 4

2 heads romaine lettuce, washed and dried
½ cup Caesar Dressing (recipe follows)
½ cup Parmesan cheese
2 cups garlic croutons

Tear lettuce leaves into long manageable strips. Place in large bowl (aluminum, wood or glass, as you wish). Add Caesar Dressing. Toss joyfully with Parmesan cheese. Add croutons (which you can make yourself, if the mood strikes you, by frying dried bread with garlic, salt and olive oil).

CAESAR DRESSING

The Caesar salad was born on a Fourth of July weekend in 1924 at Caesar Cardini's Caesar's Palace restaurant in Tijuana, Mexico. Supposedly, on this particular busy weekend, Cardini was running low on food. And so, rummaging through his icebox, he cobbled together a salad for his guests from what was left over. The salad quickly traveled north of the border, and turned into one of the most popular salads of the twentieth century. For those interested in the obtaining the dressing, bottles of Cardini's Original Caesar Dressing can be found in better markets.

Yields 2 ½ cups

1 ounce whole anchovies
1 tablespoon fresh garlic (chopped)
½ cup balsamic vinegar
1 tablespoon apple cider vinegar
½ teaspoon ground black pepper
1 tablespoon fresh lime juice
½ teaspoon Tabasco Sauce
½ teaspoon Worcestershire Sauce
1 tablespoon sherry vinegar
2 ounces Dijon mustard
2 cups virgin olive oil
salt to taste

In a mixing bowl, combine all the ingredients and blend.

TOMATILLO SAUCE

In Oaxaca, they make this wonderfully tangy sauce using *gusanos de maguey*, the tiny grubs that live in the *maguey* plant that are also used to flavor *mezcal*. At the Sonora Cafe, the Tomatillo Sauce is also wonderfully tangy, though without the addition of *gusanos de maguey*. Instead, it's the skill of the kitchen that makes this sauce so perfect with anything from chips to chicken and fish, beef and pork, and vegetables.

Yields 6 cups

3 pounds tomatillos (husked, rinsed and coarsely chopped)
10 fresh *serrano* chiles (seeded and coarsely chopped; be careful
    to wash hands after preparation to avoid burning eyes and skin)
5 medium garlic cloves (coarsely chopped)
½ cup fresh cilantro (coarsely chopped)
salt to taste

In a large nonreactive saucepan over moderate heat, combine the tomatillos and *serranos* with 4 cups water and bring to a boil. Reduce the heat to low and simmer until the tomatillos are tender. Drain, reserving 1/2 cup of the liquid.

In a blender or food processor, puree the tomatillo mixture with the garlic and cilantro and transfer to a bowl. If needed, use some of the reserved liquid to thin the sauce. Season with salt.

Note: This sauce can be prepared up to 1 day ahead. Cover and refrigerate.

"The best margaritas, the best green corn tamales, the best Mexican food I've ever had. But most of all, it's such a pleasure to dine with you because you care and all those who work with you care. *Viva* El Cholo!" – Linda Evans

COCKTAIL SAUCE

The only cocktail that cocktail sauce is used on is a seafood cocktail, usually dominated by shrimp, though crab is fairly common as well. In Mexican seafood restaurants, the sauce is poured liberally over *cocteles*, which can be massive constructs of any of a half dozen shellfish and fish. The dish should be large enough for a main course, or to be shared by two. Though the use of ketchup may seem mundane, it's essential to the flavor. And we should remember that President Ronald Reagan declared ketchup to be a vegetable. So, following his reasoning, cocktail sauce is good for you, too.

Serves 6

1 cup chili sauce
2 tablespoons fresh horseradish (grated)
1 tablespoon white vinegar
2 tablespoons lemon juice
1 cup ketchup
dash of Tabasco Sauce (½ teaspoon for spicier sauce)
salt to taste
½ teaspoon white pepper
2 tablespoons finely diced celery

In a mixing bowl, combine all the ingredients. Cover well to prevent oxidation and keep refrigerated until ready to use.

"I lived within a block of El Cholo as a kid. The address of 3054-1/2 12th St. is still there. I wrote my early stories upstairs and joined Laraine Day's little theater group. I walked by El Cholo hundreds of times on my way to some great previews at the Uptown Theater. But I could never eat there . . . no money . . . until I was in my thirties." – Ray Bradbury

ANCHO CHILE PUREE

The *ancho*, otherwise known as the *poblano*, is one of the kings of the dried chile world, a chile whose name refers to its wide, flat appearance (*ancho* means "broad"), a chile that's often as wide as it is long. The color is brownish-red, the flavor intense without necessarily being hot. The aroma of an *ancho*, once inhaled, is never forgotten.

Yields 1 cup

10 *ancho* chiles (dry)
1 tablespoon fresh lime juice
½ cup olive oil or good-quality peanut oil
salt to taste

Place the chiles in a bowl and cover with water. Place a plate on the chiles to weight them down and soak overnight or until softened. Remove and discard the stems and seeds. In a food processor, puree the flesh with the lime juice and push through a fine-mesh sieve or food mill into a bowl. Whisk in the oil and season with salt to taste.
Serve with three-cheese quesadillas.

"I first remember El Cholo in about 1929. I was attending USC. It was Prohibition. Eating out, it was customary to bring your own booze. Either bootlegged, or perhaps you returned from a weekend in Tijuana with a bottle of tequila that you kept hidden under the table. You ordered a margarita sans alcohol, and spiked it. We lived dangerously. A good dinner at El Cholo cost from fifty cents to a dollar. And El Cholo thrived. People came from all over the city to eat there. Much has changed in Los Angeles since then. But El Cholo is still tops." – Norman Cowan

ANCHO CHILE HONEY SAUCE

A remarkable marriage of flavors, combining the earthy intensity of the *ancho* with the sublime, yet highly vegetative, flavor (and aroma) of honey, a combination that works wonders in bringing out the flavors of chicken in particular. Frankly, I've often been tempted to spread the stuff on bread; this is a sauce that's finger-lickin' good. And by the way, this sauce is also excellent with lamb or salmon.

Yields 1 quart

6 *ancho* chiles (dried)
1 small red onion (quartered)
2 garlic cloves
2 cups chicken stock
1 tablespoon honey
2 tablespoons unsalted butter (¼ stick)
2 tablespoons fresh lime juice
salt
freshly ground pepper

Toast chiles in a small heavy skillet over medium heat until aromatic, turning frequently, about 5 minutes. Stem, seed and cut into small pieces. Transfer to a blender.

Preheat broiler. Grill onion and garlic on a rack for approximately 5 minutes. Transfer to blender. Add chicken stock and honey and mix to a rough puree, approximately 15 seconds. Pour mixture into a small heavy saucepan. Whisk in the butter and lime juice. Season to taste with salt and pepper. Keep sauce warm over very low heat.

PINEAPPLE-CILANTRO SALSA

A salsa that almost singlehandedly defines the variant flavors and influences of nouvelle Southwestern cooking, balancing the fire of the chiles with the intensity of the garlic and cilantro, then turning the whole concoction on its ear with the addition of pineapple. Suddenly, the whole equation is revised, the expected flavor turned around. And it tastes great, too.

Yields 3 cups

½ medium-sized pineapple (peeled, cored and cut into ½-inch cubes)
1 small onion (coarsely chopped)
1 small garlic clove (finely chopped)
1 bunch cilantro leaves (finely chopped)
½ teaspoon *pequin* chile
½ teaspoon salt
¼ teaspoon oregano
¼ teaspoon cayenne pepper

In a mixing bowl, toss together all the ingredients. Cover the bowl and chill the salsa at least 1 hour.

"He was twenty and I was eighteen. We had been broken up for over a year when he called to ask if I would see him for dinner. I said yes. Knowing that the way to a woman's heart is through her tastebuds, he chose El Cholo as our meeting place. It was raining that night and cold. As we ate, we both held our tortillas like warm blankets, not knowing what to expect. We both ordered the Number Five combination – taco and chile relleno. It was obvious. We were meant to be together." – Julie Martin

CALIFORNIA RANCHO SALSA

Not to be confused with creamy ranch dressing, this is a salsa for the twenty-first century, traditional yet on the edge of the flavor spectrum, a marvelous blend of ingredients that can become rather hot if the *jalapeños* are at the peak of flavor. Take note of the use of olive oil in many of the recipes. Olive oil is not a standard ingredient in Mexican cooking, but in the world of modern Southwestern cuisine, olive oil is as basic as it is to the cooking of Italy or Spain.

Yields 3 cups

5 ripe tomatoes (peeled, seeded and chopped)
4 Anaheim chiles (peeled, seeded and chopped)
2 *jalapeño* chiles (fresh or canned, seeded, minced; be careful to
    wash hands after peparation to avoid burning eyes and skin)
½ onion (minced)
1 clove garlic (minced)
1 to 2 tablespoons wine vinegar
2 tablespoons olive oil
salt to taste
1 teaspoon fresh oregano or ½ teaspoon dried oregano
2 to 3 tablespoons snipped cilantro
2 to 3 tablespoons tomato puree (optional)

Blister the tomatoes over a flame or plunge into boiling water for 30 seconds and then into cold water. Slip off skins.

Char the chiles over a gas flame or under a broiler until blackened. Place in a paper sack for 5 minutes to steam. Remove the skin under cold running water. Cut the tops off the chiles and remove the veins and seeds.

Combine the tomatoes and chiles with the remaining ingredients and allow the salsa to mellow in the refrigerator at least 1 hour before serving. If the salsa seems too thin, you can bind it together by stirring in a few tablespoons of tomato sauce or tomato puree. Note: This salsa keeps well for 1 day.

JALAPEÑO CORN BREAD

Jalapeño Corn Bread and Blue Corn Bread are served at the beginning of every meal at Sonora Cafe. These highly flavorful breads have been responsible for many a diner feeling full long before the first course arrives. And for good reason – the *Jalapeño* Corn Bread has a mild spiciness that makes the palate demand more and more, while the blue corn bread has a buttery sweetness that's the perfect counterpoint. Make too much – both these breads freeze very nicely.

Serves 8

⅔ cup unsalted butter
2 cups cornmeal
2 cups all-purpose flour
6 tablespoons sugar
2 tablespoons baking powder
2 teaspoons salt
2 eggs
2 cups milk
1 *jalapeño* (seeded and finely chopped. Be careful to wash hands after preparation to avoid burning eyes and skin)

Melt butter. Mix all ingredients together and place into madeleine molds. Bake at 350 degrees until fluffy, 8 to 10 minutes.

BLUE CORN BREAD

Serves 6

⅔ cup butter
2 cups blue cornmeal
2 cups white flour
6 tablespoons sugar
2 tablespoons baking powder
2 teaspoons salt
2 eggs
2 cups milk

Melt butter. Mix all ingredients together and place into madeleine molds. Bake at 350 degrees until fluffy, 8 to 10 minutes.

POT BEANS

What baked beans are to the Brahmins of Boston, pot beans are to diners at Sonora Cafe, the humble bean raised to its highest level of accomplishment. For those who have been passing on their refried beans, attention must be paid to these potted pintos. And though they can be made without lard or bacon drippings, I don't recommend it. Other oils just don't taste the same.

Serves 6

2 cups dried black, pinto or pink beans
10 cups water
¼ onion
3 tablespoons lard or bacon drippings
1 sprig *epazote*
1 tablespoon salt
3 *serrano* chiles

Rinse the beans, cover with room temperature water and let soak for at least 4 hours. Discard any beans that float, then drain.

Place the beans in a large pot or Dutch oven and add the water, onion and lard. Cook, covered, over medium heat for 2 hours or until tender. Make sure there is always enough water to cover the beans. Add more hot water if needed. When the beans are tender, uncover, add the *epazote*, salt, and chiles and cook, uncovered, 20 minutes. Add more seasonings if necessary.

> "Even though some people in our family have moved across the country, the El Cholo urge still lingers on. Whenever anyone gets off the plane to visit us, the first thing they always say is, 'I'm starved. Let's go to El Cholo.' The most extreme case of El Cholo-itis is definitely my grandmother. She lives in New York now. I'm going to visit her in a few days. She's so desperate for El Cholo food that she had my mom ask one of the managers to package a bunch of the rolled tacos for me to take to New York so Grandma can reheat them. Now that's a diehard customer!" – Sarah Harman

MEXICAN RICE

Not to be confused with Spanish rice, this rice is so good, so satisfying, it could easily be a main course in and of itself. In contrast to the overcooked, somewhat disastrous rice served in far too many Mexican restaurants, this is veritable manna from heaven. Only risotto and paella are more thoroughly satisfying – and they're both far more difficult to make.

Serves 12

⅓ pound unsalted butter
1 pound mushrooms (sliced)
1 cup onions (chopped)
1 cup corn kernels (fresh is best)
6 medium tomatoes (diced)
1 teaspoon white pepper
1 teaspoon ground cumin
2 teaspoons granulated garlic
1 tablespoon salt
4 cups tomato juice
4 cups chicken stock
1 tablespoon chicken base
4 cups long-grain white rice (fried until lightly browned)

In a saucepan, heat butter until melted. Add mushrooms, onions, corn, tomatoes, pepper, cumin, garlic and salt. Sauté briefly. Add tomato juice, chicken stock and chicken base. Bring to a boil over medium heat, then add the rice and cook until rice is soft and flaky.

Vegetables en Escabeche

A standard dish found throughout Mexico, *escabeche* refers to the act of pickling vegetables. And though the selection of vegetables here runs to carrots, onions, turnips, cauliflower, peppers and chiles, almost any other vegetable can be used. I've even tried it with mushrooms, with astounding results.

Serves 8

½ cup *jalapeño* vinegar
2 cups white vinegar
2 cups rice vinegar
1 bunch cilantro (stems off)
½ head of whole garlic
½ cup water
¼ cup sugar
1 tablespoon salt
1 carrot (sliced)
¼ onion (sliced)
¾ turnip (cut into sticks)
¼ head cauliflower (cut into pieces)
¼ each red, green and yellow bell pepper (sliced)
⅛ pound green *jalapeños*
⅛ pound red *jalapeños*
⅛ pound *serrano* chiles

In a saucepan, bring vinegars, cilantro, garlic, water, sugar and salt to a boil. Add carrot, onion, turnip and cauliflower. Boil 1 more minute, then add the bell peppers and chiles.

Remove saucepan from heat. Place in covered dish and chill until ready to serve. Note: This will keep in the refrigerator for up to 3 days.

OPEN-FACE PORTOBELLO MUSHROOM SANDWICH

Talk about thoroughly modern cuisine. This dish combines three of the hottest ingredients of the '90s – portobello mushrooms, arugula and goat cheese. Yet there's nothing pretentious about the result – this is the sort of sandwich that, as the chef points out, should be eaten with a pickle or potato chips. As fancy as it may seem, a sandwich is still a sandwich.

Serves 6

6 extra large portobello mushrooms (stems removed)
1 red onion (optional, thinly sliced and marinated with the mushrooms)
½ cup virgin olive oil
¼ cup fresh lime juice
2 tablespoons fresh basil (minced)
1 teaspoon rosemary (minced)
1 teaspoon oregano (minced)
1 teaspoon black pepper
1 teaspoon garlic (minced)
1 teaspoon salt
2 red bell peppers
6 ounces goat cheese (room temperature)
6 rosemary buns or brioche
2 vine-ripened tomatoes (sliced)
3 small bunches arugula

Marinate the portobello mushrooms (and onion if desired) with the olive oil, lime juice, basil, rosemary, oregano, black pepper, garlic and salt up to 2 hours only.

Roast the peppers over an open flame until their skin becomes black, turning frequently. Place in a paper bag or food storage bag and steam for 20 minutes. Peel the skin with your fingers; remove seeds and ribs.

Grill the mushrooms. Spread the goat cheese on the bottom of a split bun. Assemble the sandwich with tomatoes, arugula, sliced onion, roasted peppers and mushrooms.

Serve with homemade potato chips or kosher dill pickle.

CHILE RELLENO

This is a good time to put aside all the beliefs an endless number of chile relleno and enchilada combination plates have left you with. A properly made chile relleno is not a soggy, somewhat tasteless mass buried under cheese and beans. It's a delight, a remarkably focused dish in which the chiles of whatever stripe and hue play off the cheeses within and the sauces that surround them. At Sonora Cafe, the chiles rellenos are triumphs. Try both the recipe below and the *poblano* version that follows. You will become a relleno fanatic, I'm sure.

Serves 12 (1 per person)

12 *poblano* chiles (roasted, peeled and seeded)
2 pounds grated cheddar cheese
2 pounds grated Monterey Jack cheese
1 teaspoon oregano
1 teaspoon black pepper
1 teaspoon fresh basil
flour for dusting
12 eggs (separated)
pinch of salt
1 tablespoon flour
1 tablespoon baking powder
Red Chile Sauce (recipe follows)

Wrap the chile stems in foil to protect them. Place chiles on rack of hot barbecue grill or over an open flame, turning frequently with tongs, until skin is nicely blistered, charred and loosened. Place in a food storage plastic bag and steam for 10 minutes. Remove from bag, slit chiles open and remove seeds and veins, leaving stems on if possible. Rinse under cold running water, pat dry on paper towels and set aside while preparing remainder of ingredients.

In a bowl, mix cheeses, oregano, pepper and basil together. Stuff chiles and dust with flour.

To make the batter, whip egg whites until they peak. Mix in yolks, salt, flour and baking powder. Dip chiles in batter and fry in oil at 350 degrees until light brown on both sides. Place Red Chile Sauce in center of plate, then chile relleno on top.

RED CHILE SAUCE

Yields 6 cups

4 ounces olive oil
1 cup onion (diced)
1 tablespoon garlic (chopped)
1 teaspoon oregano
1 teaspoon cumin
1 teaspoon black pepper
1 teaspoon *ancho* chile paste or powder
1 tablespoon *guajillo* paste
1 quart fresh tomato puree
1 cup chicken stock
salt to taste

In a saucepan, heat the olive oil and sauté the onion and garlic. Add oregano, cumin, black pepper, *ancho* and *guajillo* pastes and cook 3 minutes. Add tomato puree and chicken stock and continue cooking 10 to 15 minutes.

Note: To make *ancho* paste and *guajillo* paste, wash and dry the chiles. Cut the chiles open and remove the stems and seeds (be careful to wash hands after preparation to avoid burning eyes and skin). Dry-roast the chiles in a skillet until they puff up, about 1 to 2 minutes. Transfer to a bowl, cover with warm water, and submerge 30 minutes. Place chiles in a blender with enough of their soaking liquid to produce a puree. Strain through a medium or fine strainer.

To make powder, again, slit open the chiles and remove the seeds. Place chiles on a baking sheet and roast 3 to 5 minutes in a preheated 300 degree oven. Crumble chiles in a bowl and grind them into a powder with a spice grinder or anything that will create a fine powder. The powder can be kept tightly covered for up to 1 month.

POBLANO CHILE RELLENO WITH RED BELL PEPPER SAUCE

Serves 6 to 8 (1 per person)

6 to 8 medium *poblano* chiles (roasted and seeded)
4 eggs (separated)
¼ teaspoon baking powder
¼ teaspoon salt
1 cup crumbled goat cheese (5 ½-ounce package)
1 cup grated fontina cheese
1 cup grated Parmesan cheese
flour for dredging chiles
oil for frying
Red Bell Pepper Sauce (recipe follows)
cilantro for garnish

Wrap the chile stems in foil to protect them. Place the chiles on a rack of a hot barbecue grill or open flame of burner, turning frequently with tongs until the skin is nicely blistered, charred and loosened. Place in a food storage bag and steam for 10 minutes. Remove from bag, slit chiles open and remove seeds and veins, leaving stems on if possible. Rinse under cold running water, pat dry on paper towels and set aside while preparing remainder of ingredients.

In a mixing bowl, beat egg yolks until thick and light in color. In a second bowl and with clean beaters, beat egg whites until stiff but not dry. Gently fold egg yolks into whites along with baking powder and salt.

In a large skillet, add cooking oil to the depth of about 1 inch. Heat over medium high heat to 375 degrees, using a deep-fat thermometer. Dredge chiles in flour, then dip into batter, coating well on all sides. Gently place chile in hot oil and cook until golden on both sides. Transfer to paper towel to drain, then arrange on warmed serving platter or individual plates. Serve with Red Bell Pepper Sauce and garnish with fresh cilantro.

RED BELL PEPPER SAUCE

Yields 3 cups

⅓ cup unsalted butter
4 red bell peppers (seeded and diced)
2 tomatoes (diced)
½ branch fresh dill weed (use dried if necessary)
⅓ cup unsalted butter (melted)
salt to taste

In a large skillet over medium heat, melt 1/3 cup butter. Add the diced peppers and tomatoes and cook 10 minutes, stirring occasionally, until soft. Transfer mixture to a food processor or blender and add the dill and the additional 1/3 cup melted butter and process to a coarse puree. The sauce should have some texture to it. Taste and season with salt. Serve with the *poblano* chile rellenos.

"I grew up with El Cholo. I started when I was fourteen years old. Which was a funny thing to do for a kid named Salisbury, because Salisbury certainly doesn't rhyme with enchilada. But our roots were in the Southwest nonetheless. In the early days of Los Angeles when we'd just arrived from Arizona, my brother George got a job as a dishwasher, a part-time dishwasher in the original El Cholo on South Broadway. That was probably 1926, a long time ago, when it was still called the Sonora Cafe. Then he and the boss's daughter fell in love with each other and they wanted to get married. He prevailed upon our widowed mother to borrow on her home. She borrowed six hundred dollars and that's what they used to start El Cholo. I used to ride my bicycle from Thirtieth Street School to the restaurant to wash pots and pans after school. And I think my compensation was a bowl of beans or a bowl of rice at the time. I don't remember, but it sure did taste good. I did that for some time until I was promoted to be a waiter. And when I knew how to do that, I went on to manage the place. Back then, all you had to do to succeed was put out a sign that said 'Mexican food' on it, and you could make money. When we first started we had a choice of tortillas or bread with the meal. And the meal at that time was fifty cents which included hors d'oeuvres, veg-

GOAT CHEESE QUESADILLA

The quesadilla is such a simple dish. And such a terribly abused one. It's hard to believe the degree to which a tortilla, stuffed and folded and fried in oil, is abused. But it is, often emerging from the kitchen looking a bit like something that's been run over by a steamroller. One of the pleasures of the quesadillas at Sonora Cafe is that they have loft, they have substance . . . and most important, they have flavor.

Serves 12

¼ pound unsalted butter
2 cups sliced leeks
20 ounces goat cheese
1 teaspoon toasted cumin
1 teaspoon toasted Mexican oregano
12 flour tortillas
Red Chile Sauce (see page 118)
cilantro
chopped chives

Melt butter, add leeks and sauté until tender.

In the meantime, cream the goat cheese. Add the leeks, cumin and oregano, and whip for about 2 minutes.

Heat tortillas. Spread each with 1 1/2 ounces of goat cheese mixture and fold tortilla over. Bake at 325 degrees about 5 minutes. Serve hot with Red Chile Sauce over half the quesadilla. Garnish with cilantro and chopped chives.

etable soup, a choice of entree with rice and beans, and a drink. And that was all one could eat. People ordered bread most of the time because they didn't know what tortillas were -- I think they were suspicious. Time went by so quickly. I remember I'd be cashiering, and a man would stand before me, tall with greying hair and say, 'I used to come in here when I was a little boy.' I'd hear that time and time and time again. And then they'd bring their children in." -- Jimmy Salisbury, who was part of the bedrock upon which El Cholo was built. Jimmy helped run El Cholo for more than 45 years, until his death in 1994.

DUCK TAMALE WITH RED CHILE SAUCE

Though widely available, duck has long been perceived as a special occasion dish. Chicken is for everyday meals, but duck is for celebrations. And since tamales are for celebrations as well, this is a doubly celebratory creation, heavy with the musky richness of duck, wonderfully gamey, irresistibly good.

Serves 18

three 4 ½-pound ducks
3 tablespoons kosher salt
1 ½ teaspoons whole black pepper
1 ½ teaspoons thyme
1 ½ teaspoons ground allspice
1 ½ teaspoons juniper berries
1 ½ teaspoons whole oregano
6 cloves garlic
3 whole *guajillo* chiles
3 teaspoons whole rosemary
40 corn husks (soak in water for 30 minutes to make pliable,
    tear 1 into strips for ties)
Red Chile Sauce (recipe on page 118)
Masa Mix (recipe follows)

Cut duck into pieces, salt and marinate with all spices and chiles 24 hours.

Bake duck in its own fat with all the ingredients for 1 1/2 hours at 250 degrees. Let the duck cool. Shred over heat.

Add chile sauce, reserving some to plate each tamale, and *pico de gallo* (diced onions, cilantro, tomatoes, lime juice and 1 *serrano* chile), mix all together and bring to a boil. Put mixture over duck. Divide the masa evenly between two overlapping corn husks. Divide the duck meat evenly and place the filling on top, roll and tie the tamales and steam about 30 minutes. Let cool slightly and serve.

MASA MIX

12 ounces vegetable shortening
3 pounds masa
1 ½ tablespoons baking powder
3 tablespoons salt
1 ½ tablespoons white pepper
1 ½ cups water

In a mixer, use the wire attachment to start mixing shortening until fluffy. Change to the paddle attachment and add masa, little by little. Last, add baking powder, salt, pepper and water; mix well for 5 minutes. Place masa in a bowl.

"Our waitress was Anita. She was young, pretty and personable. Our three children, who were there for the first time and wary of Mexican food, ordered hamburgers. Anita put on an Oscar-winning performance, blasting them in a torrent of rapid Spanish. Then her voice softened and she explained in English that they were in a Mexican restaurant and they should eat Mexican food. She said she would bring them things they would absolutely love. And she did. And they did. That was over forty years ago. I always give a silent '*Salud*' to Anita." – Rosalie Rubin

TEXAS BARBECUE DOUBLE PORK CHOP WITH SWEET POTATO TAMALE AND MANGO-PAPAYA SALSA

It's the rare recipe in which the word "Texas" isn't followed by the word "barbecue." This particular recipe breaks with the usual Texas taste for beef, using southeastern-oriented pork as the protein of choice in a dish that looks daunting (there are many parts here), but guarantees astonishing satisfaction. Remember to make the BBQ sauce in quantity; you'll find it goes well on just about anything.

Serves 10 to 12

Two 7- to 9-rib pork loin roasts
BBQ Sauce (recipe follows)
Tropical Mango-Papaya Salsa (recipe follows)

Have the butcher "French" the bone ends of pork roasts. Remove the pork from the refrigerator 1 hour before roasting. Wipe with a damp cloth and cover the bones with aluminum foil. Rub with salt and pepper.

Preheat the oven to 350 degrees. Place pork in oven and immediately reduce temperature to 325 degrees. Bake 30 minutes per pound, about 3 hours total, or until you reach a temperature of 160 degrees on a meat thermometer. Remove the roasts from the oven and cut into double-chop portions. Rub with barbecue sauce and broil the pork chops on a rack 4 inches from heat source about 8 minutes; turn and baste frequently.

BBQ SAUCE

Yields 2 quarts

1 small jicama (peeled and sliced)
1 red bell pepper (halved and seeded)
1 small onion (sliced)
3 cloves garlic (chopped)
1 celery stalk (chopped)
3 *pasilla* chiles (dry, halved and seeded)
3 *guajillo* chiles (dry, halved and seeded)
2 roma tomatoes (quartered)
2 whole *jalapeño*s (halved and seeded; be careful to wash your
    hands after preparation to avoid burning eyes and skin)
1 quart Veal Stock (recipe follows; canned beef broth can be sub-
    stituted if necessary)
1 teaspoon dried mustard
⅓ cup raspberry wine vinegar
⅓ cup brown sugar
1 tablespoon molasses
1 teaspoon fresh ginger (chopped)
3 whole cloves
¼ teaspoon liquid smoke
1 tablespoon tomato paste
dash of Tabasco sauce
½ cup ketchup
kosher salt

Smoke all the vegetables and chiles about 20 minutes (see "Preparing the Smoker"). Transfer the ingredients to a medium saucepan with the Veal Stock. Bring to a boil and reduce the liquid by 1/3. Whisk in the mustard, strain and set aside.

In a small saucepan, whisk together the vinegar, sugar, molasses, ginger, cloves, liquid smoke, tomato paste and Tabasco. Bring to a boil and continue cooking until the mixture becomes syrupy, about 3 minutes. Add to the strained veal stock mixture and whisk in the ketchup. Strain the BBQ sauce through a fine mesh strainer and season with koksher salt to taste.

PREPARING THE SMOKER

Home smokers are available from specialty hardware stores and mail-order sources. They are relatively inexpensive, so they are well worth the investment. You can also adapt a barbecue by adding a pan of water to the bottom, sealing all but one vent, and follow the method described below.

Soak 6 to 8 chunks of aromatic hardwood, such as hickory, mesquite or apple in water 20 minutes. Place a pan of water in the bottom of the smoker. Build a fire in the smoker with hardwood lamp charcoal or charcoal briquettes and an electric starter. Let the charcoal burn down until it is covered by a uniform whitish-gray ash, which should take 20 to 30 minutes, and spread the coals out. Add the soaked hardwood chunks and let burn 5 minutes. Place the ingredients to be smoked on the grill over the water pan and cover with the top of the smoker. Stoke the fire every 30 minutes, adding more charcoal and soaked wood chunks as necessary. As a general rule, an average chicken of 2 1/2 pounds will take 1 1/2 hours to 2 hours at a temperature of 250 degrees. Chicken or duck breast will take 20 to 25 minutes. Tomatoes will take 20 minutes. Chiles, bell peppers and onions will take 25 to 30 minutes.

VEAL STOCK

Yields ½ gallon

4 pounds veal bones
2 ounces oil
3 quarts cold water
½ pound *mirepoix* (mixture of chopped onion, carrots, celery)
3 ounces tomato paste
***bouquet garni* (2 parsley stems, ¼ teaspoon thyme leaves, 1 bay**
    leaf, ¼ teaspoon cracked peppercorns)
salt (optional)

Rinse the bones and dry them well. Brown the bones in the oil. Combine the bones and water. Bring the water to a boil over low heat. Simmer for a total of about 6 hours, skimming the surface as necessary. Brown the *mirepoix* and tomato paste. Add to the stock after the stock has simmered about 5 hours. Deglaze the reduced drippings with water and add to the stock. Add *bouquet garni* and salt if desired. Simmer an additional hour. Strain the stock.

TROPICAL MANGO-PAPAYA SALSA

2 papayas (peeled, seeded and cut into large dice)
2 mangos (peeled, pitted and diced)
1 tablespoon red bell pepper (seeded and minced)
1 tablespoon fresh basil (minced)
¼ cup fresh lime juice
1 tablespoon fresh ginger (minced)
1 teaspoon maple syrup
2 *serrano* chiles (seeded and minced; be careful to wash hands
    after preparation to avoid burning eyes and skin)

In a mixing bowl, thoroughly combine all the ingredients. This mildly hot salsa is also excellent with pork or firm fresh fish or cheese quesadillas.

TAMALES DE CAMOTE DULCE

A true *camote* is the best, but the common sweet potato (not a yam, which is reddish-orange), which is yellowish, works well. These light tamales also make a great appetizer.

Yields 6 tamales

1 quart water
3 small (6 to 8 ounces) sweet potatoes (peeled and cut into small
    chunks, about 3 cups)
⅓ cup *piloncillo* (Mexican brown sugar) or brown sugar
⅓ cup pure maple syrup
⅓ cup unsalted butter
½ teaspoon ground cinnamon
¼ teaspoon ground cloves

In a saucepan, put the water, sweet potatoes, brown sugar, maple syrup, butter, cinnamon and cloves, and bring to a boil over medium-high heat. Reduce the heat and simmer about 15 minutes, until the potatoes are just tender. Strain the potatoes and reserve the cooking liquid for the masa dough.

MASA DOUGH FOR SWEET POTATO TAMALES

Yields dough for 6 tamales

2 medium sweet potatoes
4 cups water
1 cup vegetable shortening (at room temperature)
3 cups fresh masa or masa harina
½ cup cornmeal
1 teaspoon baking powder
¼ teaspoon cayenne chile powder
¼ teaspoon ground cumin
1 tablespoon salt
1 ¼ cups cooked sweet potato
2 cups reserved potato cooking liquid
16 corn husks (soaked in hot water 30 minutes or until pliable, using 2 to make 16 strips for ties)

Combine sweet potatoes and water in a pot and boil until potatoes are soft. Reserve liquid.

In the bowl of an electric mixer, whisk the vegetable shortening until light and fluffy. Scrape down the sides of the bowl as necessary.

In a separate bowl, combine the dry ingredients and sweet potato, reserving 3/4 cup of sweet potato, and gradually add the reserved potato cooking liquid. Mix to form a soft dough. Add the dough to the shortening while whisking until the mixture becomes quite sticky.

Drain the corn husks and pat dry. Place 2 husks together with the large ends overlapping by 2 inches. Repeat for the remaining husks. Divide the tamale dough evenly among the double husks and spread in the center, leaving 1 inch at each end uncovered. Place the reserved 3/4 cup sweet potatoes, mashed, on top of the masa dough. Roll the corn husks so the filling is completely enclosed. Twist and tie each end with the ties from the corn husks.

Steam the tamales in a conventional steamer or in a strainer or vegetable basket set in a saucepan of boiling water and cover with a tight-fitting lid. It is important that little or no steam escapes while cooking. Steam 30 to 35 minutes. The water should always be lightly boiling. The tamales are done when the dough comes away easily from the husk.

When cooked, slice the tamales from end to end. Push the ends gently together as for a baked potato. Serve with the Mango-Papaya Salsa and the BBQ Sauce on the side.

ROCK SALT-BAKED PRINCE EDWARD ISLAND MUSSELS WITH CILANTRO-*JALAPEÑO* MAYONNAISE AND DRAWN BUTTER

Though the chef prefers Prince Edward Island mussels, I've found that New Zealand green lips work quite nicely as well. Of course almost anything, including my sneakers, would taste good slathered with Cilantro-*Jalapeño* Mayonnaise, which may be the best mayonnaise in the world. Once again, be sure to make extra; you'll find lots of uses for the stuff, including licking it off the spoon.

Serves 6

6 pounds Prince Edward Island Mussels
3 green Anaheim chiles (seeded and sliced into rings)
3 red Anaheim chiles (seeded and sliced into rings)
½ cup kosher salt (or to taste, about 1 tablespoon per serving)
1 bunch cilantro (stems off)
1 pound unsalted clarified butter for dipping
Cilantro-*Jalapeño* Mayonnaise for dipping (recipe follows)

The rules for preparing the mussels are simple. Live mussels usually keep their shells tightly closed, so when collecting your own, discard those with open shells. However, mussels will "gape" if exposed to temperature changes, such as when moved from the refrigerator to room temperature. To test these for freshness, hold the mussel between your thumb and forefinger and press laterally as though sliding the two shells across one another. If the shell moves, the mussel is not fresh. A live mussel will remain rigid. Each mussel must be thoroughly scrubbed with a wire brush or plastic pot scrubber to remove the mud and grass that clings to the shell, as well as the "beard." After cooking, be sure to discard any mussels that have not opened their shells. Divide into 6 equal portions or about 20 to 24 mussels each.

In a stainless steel bowl, toss in the mussels with the chiles, salt and cilantro. Transfer to a cast-iron skillet and bake at 400 degrees 5 minutes or until they all open. Serve with clarified butter and Cilantro-*Jalapeño* Mayonnaise.

CILANTRO-JALAPEÑO MAYONNAISE

Yields 2 ½ cups

2 cloves garlic (chopped)
2 ½ cups cilantro (leaves only)
1 teaspoon sugar
1 teaspoon salt
½ teaspoon white pepper
1 teaspoon rice vinegar
2 egg yolks
1 tablespoon fresh lime juice
1 *jalapeño* chile (seeded and chopped; be careful to wash hands
   after preparation to avoid burning eyes and skin)
1 cup extra-virgin olive oil
¾ cup walnut oil

Place all the ingredients, except the oils, in a blender. Blend while adding the oils in a steady stream. Continue to blend until smooth.

Leftover mayonnaise can be used with fried oysters or grilled fish. It can be stored tightly covered in the refrigerator. Note: as most cooks are aware, there are warnings against the use of raw eggs in any recipe.

Scallops Ceviche

The "cooking" technique known as *ceviche* is often credited to the Incas, who discovered that seafood would change in texture and flavor when marinated in lemon or lime juice. It's a remarkably simple process to accomplish at home, for there's no need to go anywhere near the stove. Once you prepare the seafood, you simply pour over the juice, and then go away for a while. When you return – shazam! – the dish is triumphantly good.

Serves 4

¾ to 1 pound fresh scallops
1 cup lime juice to cover
2 cloves garlic (finely chopped)
1 sweet red bell pepper or Anaheim chile (deveined, seeded and julienned)
½ bunch coriander or cilantro (stemmed and coarsely chopped)
1 large tomato (cored and chopped)
2 *jalapeño* chiles (with seeds, finely chopped; be careful to wash hands after preparation to avoid burning eyes and skin)
½ cup olive oil

Uniformly slice the scallops into thirds, preserving the shape. Place in bowl, add lime juice and marinate 1 hour. Add garlic, red bell pepper or green chile. Mix thoroughly. Add coriander, tomato, and *jalapeño* chiles. Add olive oil, mix well and serve immediately. Do not keep more than 2 to 3 hours.

CORN CHOWDER WITH JALAPEÑO CREAM

I like to think of this dish as the first example of a new style of "blendo" cooking – New England/Southwestern. Indeed, were it not for the presence of the *Jalapeño* Cream, it would be pure New England. But the cream turns the whole recipe upside down. And it works, striking a blow for New Regionalism. Can a Southwestern clambake be far behind?

Serves 6

6 pounds littleneck clams in shell
1 cup white wine
3 cups chicken stock
1 clove garlic
2 sprigs thyme
7 ears of fresh corn (shucked)
butter
1 small onion (medium dice)
1 small carrot (medium dice)
1 stalk celery (medium dice)
1 small leek (medium dice)
1 ½ cups cream
juice of ¼ lemon
salt and pepper

Make sure the clamshells are tightly closed. Discard any clams with opened shells. Scrub shells thoroughly with a wire brush.

Bring white wine and chicken stock to a boil. Add garlic, thyme and clams. Cook until clams are just opened. Strain, saving liquid. Set clams aside.

Remove corn kernels from cobs, set cobs aside and reserve 1/2 cup kernels for garnish.

In a 3-quart saucepan, heat butter and sauté onion, carrot, celery and leek until tender. Add clam liquid and bring to a boil. Add corn and cobs and simmer 20 to 30 minutes. Remove cobs. Strain, reserving liquid. Place remaining vegetables in a blender. Add cream, lemon juice, salt and pepper and puree. Add to reserved liquid.

Bring soup to a boil. Adjust seasoning. Remove clams from shells and add to soup, reserving a few for garnish.

JALAPEÑO CREAM

Yields 2 cups

2 *jalapeño* peppers (seeds removed; be careful to wash hands
    after preparation to avoid burning eyes and skin)
½ cup sour cream
1 cup whipping cream
½ bunch cilantro (finely chopped)

    Fold all ingredients together and season to taste with salt, pepper and lemon juice.

    To present the dish, serve in individual bowls of about 7 ounces of soup and 2 teaspoons of *Jalapeño* Cream. Garnish with a few clams and several corn kernels.

"El Cholo was crowded, but after a short wait we were shown to our table in the central courtyard. When my father-in-law sat down, the late afternoon sun was shining into his eyes through an opening in the ceiling. Our waiter assured us that he would take care of everything. The next thing we knew one of the busboys was crawling across the roof with a hammer, nails and board. Within a minute or so, he located the offending opening and nailed a board over it." – Douglas Elwell

GAZPACHO

Most people perceive gazpacho as nothing more than cold tomato juice flavored with chopped-up vegetables. Which, at its worst, it often is. But at its best, as in the case of the gazpacho prepared at Sonora Cafe, it's a paean to the pleasures of cold flavors, which change in intensity as they change in temperature. The use of clam juice in particular seriously affects the equation, turning this into a soup of many layers. You taste something different with every spoonful.

Serves 6

½ Anaheim chile (roasted, peeled and seeded)
2 large ripe tomatoes (chopped)
½ large onion (chopped)
¼ garlic clove (chopped)
½ cucumber (peeled, seeded and chopped)
2 cups tomato juice
1 cup clam juice
¼ cup white wine vinegar
¾ teaspoon olive oil
¼ cup dry white wine
1 teaspoon paprika
½ teaspoon salt
¼ teaspoon ground black pepper
¼ teaspoon ground cumin
a few dashes Worcestershire Sauce
a few dashes of Tabasco
1 avocado (diced)

Roast the Anaheim chile over an open flame, turning frequently, until the skins blackens. Place in a paper bag or food storage bag and steam 20 minutes. Peel skin with your hands, remove seeds and stem.

In a large bowl, place the tomatoes, onion, garlic, cucumber and chile. Pour tomato juice over mixture and let stand 2 hours. Add clam juice, vinegar, oil, wine, paprika, salt, pepper, cumin, Worcestershire and Tabasco. Whirl in a blender until smooth. Strain through sieve and chill several hours. Add cold water if too thick. Serve in soup cups with diced avocado.

CAPIROTADA

In classic bread pudding, stale (or not stale) bread is saturated with milk, eggs, sugar and spices, then baked. In the classic Mexican *capirotada*, much is added to make it a sort of super bread pudding – honey, fresh fruits, the stick cinnamon called *canela*, nuts, dried fruit, cheese, even tomatoes and onions. In the case of the version made at the Sonora Cafe, there are raisins, apples, apricots and butterscotch sauce. Very indulgent, very sweet, and very, very good.

Serves 10 to 12

1 loaf brioche or French bread
Glazed Dried Apricots (recipe follows), diced
1 Golden Delicious apple (cored, peeled and shredded)
½ cup raisins
Butterscotch Sauce (recipe follows)
Custard (recipe follows)
2 cups unsweetened whipping cream

Preheat oven to 325 degrees. Trim the crust off brioche or French bread loaf. Slice bread into 1/2-inch-thick slices. Place bread slices to cover bottom of buttered 10 x 13-inch glass baking dish. Do not overlap. Mix diced apricots with shredded apples. Sprinkle half of apricot-apple mixture over the bread, then half of the raisins. Pour a third of butterscotch over bread. Pour half of custard. Place another layer of bread as before. Top with remaining half of apricot-apple mixture and raisins, 1/3 butterscotch and remaining custard. Arrange bread to cover once again, and top with butterscotch. Bake for 1 hour. If *capirotada* starts to get too brown on top, cover loosely with foil and continue baking until the custard is set. (Skewer inserted into custard should come out clean.) Let *capirotada* cool 20 minutes and serve with unsweetened whipping cream.

BUTTERSCOTCH SAUCE

1 ½ cups brown sugar
¼ cup water
6 tablespoons unsalted butter
1 ½ cups whipping cream
1 tablespoon cider vinegar

Combine the sugar and water in a 3-quart saucepan. Stir over low heat until the sugar dissolves, then increase heat to medium and bring to a boil. Let butterscotch sauce cool for a few minutes. Return to burner on low to medium heat. Slowly add butter, stirring continuously, until mixture has been at a rolling boil for 2 minutes. Add cream and vinegar, stirring continuously, and boil for 1 more minute. Set aside until ready to use.

GLAZED DRIED APRICOTS

2 cups sugar
1 cup water
½ pound dried apricots

Bring sugar and water to a boil. Add dried apricots, reduce heat to low and simmer 20 minutes. Let apricots cool in syrup. Drain remaining syrup from apricots (most will absorb).

CUSTARD

6 whole eggs
3 ounces sugar
3 ounces flour
1 quart 40% heavy cream

Mix eggs in bowl. Add sugar, flour and cream. Set aside.

FLAN

Though flan originated in Spain, it's every bit as ubiquitous in Mexico, and every bit as appealing. This is a dessert that's especially well suited to cooling the palate after a meal filled with spice and intensity. The only problem I have with flan is that I can't seem to stop eating the stuff. I have no self control – I believe myself a flanoholic.

Serves 10

2 cups sugar
5 tablespoons water
1 quart milk
6 eggs
6 ½ ounces sugar
½ ounce vanilla extract

To make caramel, in a small heavy saucepan over high heat, stir together the sugar and water. Bring to a boil and cook, without stirring, until the mixture turns mahogany brown, about 5 to 8 minutes. Immediately pour into custard cups and set aside to harden.

Heat milk until it just comes to a boil. Whisk the eggs and sugar together and slowly temper the eggs with the milk to avoid scrambling the eggs. Pour in the rest of the milk and stir in the vanilla. Strain.

Pour into custard cups over caramel.

Bake in *bain marie*, or pan of hot water bath that comes halfway up the sides of the custard cups and bake 45 minutes to 1 hour at 375 degrees. After about 15 minutes of baking, you may cover the flans with foil.

CHOCOLATE PRALINE CAKE

The praline in this recipe is a crunchy confection made of almonds and caramelized sugar. It's flavor is overwhelmingly sweet, so it works far better as an ingredient in Sonora Cafe's Chocolate Praline Cake.

Serves 12

½ cup sugar
½ cup water
12 ounces chocolate
8 ounces butter
½ cup almond meal
6 eggs (at room temperature)
⅓ cup sugar
Praline Buttercream (recipe follows)

Preheat oven to 350 degrees. Combine 1/2 cup sugar and water and heat to simple syrup and slightly thick. Stir in chocolate and butter until melted. Stir in almond meal. Whip eggs and 1/3 cup sugar until ribbon forms when beaters are lifted. Combine both mixtures and pour into pan well greased on bottom and sides. Bake 1 hour in *bain marie*, or pan of hot water that comes halfway up sides of pan. Let cool 20 to 30 minutes before removing from pan. Chill well and frost with Praline Buttercream.

PRALINE BUTTERCREAM

1 pound sugar
½ cup water
1 egg
2 egg yolks
1 quart 40% heavy cream
4 ounces praline
3 sticks butter

Cook sugar and water to 238 degrees on candy thermometer. Whip egg and yolks until very light. Slowly add syrup while whipping in blender. Whip until cool. Slowly add praline, then butter. Whip until very light and fluffy. Refrigerate until ready to use. Rewhip before use. This will store in the refrigerator 1 week.

WHITE CHOCOLATE-RICE PUDDING TAMALES WITH MYERS'S RUM CREAM

Chocolate may be the finest culinary achievement of Mexico (and that's saying much, considering how many ingredients Mexico brings to the world's table). In this case, it's a tamale, it's a pudding, it's a chocolate bar. It's staggeringly good, without being devastatingly sweet. It's an excellent conclusion to any meal. Or to no meal at all – what better than a margarita and a chocolate-rice pudding tamale to finish off a day?

Serves 12

2 cups long-grain white rice (soaked in 3 cups water 2 hours or
    overnight)
1 quart milk
1 cup half and half
2 8-ounce cans sweetened condensed milk
1 teaspoon ground cinnamon
1 cup sugar
¾ cup raisins
2 cups grated white chocolate
1 teaspoon vanilla extract (essence)
ground cinnamon for garnish (optional)
25 corn husks (covered in warm water until pliable)
Myers's Rum Cream (recipe follows)
Grated white chocolate for garnish (optional)

Drain and place the rice in a large saucepan with the milk, half and half and condensed milk, cinnamon and sugar. Bring to a boil, lower the heat and cook, covered, until most of the milk has been absorbed, stirring constantly until the mixture thickens. Add the raisins and vanilla and cook 2 minutes. Transfer to a platter or bowl and refrigerate. Mix in the grated white chocolate or sprinkle on top with cinnamon if served in individual bowls.

To make the tamales, drain the corn husks and pat dry. Tear 12 1/4-inch strips from one husk for ties.

Place two husks together with large ends overlapping by about 2 inches. Spread about a tablespoon of the rice pudding mixture down the middle of the corn husk, leaving 1 inch at each end uncovered.

Roll the corn husk so that the filling is completely enclosed (as for a crepe), twist and tie each end of the tamale with the ties from the corn husk. Repeat process for remaining tamales.

Place tamales in a steamer over gently boiling water and steam 5 to 7 minutes. Remove, slice tamales with a knife from end to end and push together like a baked potato. Pour some of the Myers's Rum Cream over each tamale and garnish with grated white chocolate.

MYERS'S RUM CREAM

2 egg yolks
½ cup sugar
2 cups heavy cream
1 tablespoon Myers's Dark Rum

In a mixing bowl, beat the egg yolks and sugar together and set aside. In a saucepan, bring the cream and rum to a boil and pour half of the mixture into the yolk mixture slowly to temper the eggs. Beating vigorously, put the remaining cream mixture back into the pan over the heat. Slowly pour the tempered egg yolk mixture into the saucepan and whisk vigorously until incorporated. Cook until the mixture smoothly coats the back of a spoon, about 5 minutes. Strain and cool.

THANK YOU! COME AGAIN!

·INDEX·

About the Author & the Designer

Merrill Shindler has been writing and speaking about the pleasures of the palate for most of his adult life. An affably eccentric host on Los Angeles radio, he is the co-editor of the best-selling *Zagat Los Angeles Restaurant Survey* and author of *American Dish: 100 Recipes from Ten Delicious Decades*. He describes himself as "just a big ol' hungry boy" who spends his spare time trying to figure out where to eat next. As he candidly admits, he returns most often to El Cholo.

Dave Matli, a graphic artist for more than two years, working on corporate design and collateral, has only recently entered the world of publishing. The *El Cholo Cookbook* marks his second book independently designed. He hopes that it will appeal to the senses as much as the recipes do.

When visiting Southern California, enjoy the fine food of the El Cholo family of restaurants:

El Cholo Restaurant, 1121 South Western Ave., Los Angeles

Sonora Cafe, 180 South La Brea Ave., Los Angeles

The Cat & The Custard Cup, 800 East Whittier Blvd., Whittier

Cafe El Cholo, 840 East Whittier Blvd., Whittier

El Cholo Santa Monica, 1025 Wilshire Blvd., Santa Monica

Spanish-Mexican Dishes

SOUPS

ALBONDIGAS (Spanish Meat Ball Soup)...................35c

" (½ Order).................................20c

VEGETABLE SOUP 10c

RELISHES

Combination Salad.................30c
Sliced Tomatoes..................20c
Hearts of Lettuce................15c
Mex. Pickled Peppers
or Onions 10c

DRINKS

Coffee ...... 5c Tea 10c
Milk ......10c Choc. 10c
Draught Beer 10c
Local Bottle Beer 15c
Dry Ginger Ale 25c

45¢
12:00 to 3:00 P.M.
Special Plate Lunch
VEGETABLE SOUP
Choice of One:
ENCHILADA   TAMALE
CHILE CON CARNE
with
FRIED BEANS
and
RICE or SPAGHETTI
TORTILLAS or BREAD
Coffee
Glass Beer   Glass Claret

60¢
Combination Plate
SOUP
Albondigas or Vegetable
Choice of One
ENCHILADA
CHILE RELLENO   TAMALE
CHILE CON CARNE
with
FRIED BEANS
and
RICE or SPAGHETTI
TORTILLAS or BREAD
Coffee or Milk
Glass Beer   Glass Claret

EL CHOLO SPANISH CAFES — LOS ANGELES, 4012 SO.
ORDERS TO TAKE OUT